PEACE,
POLITICS,
AND THE PEOPLE OF GOD

PEACE,
POLITICS,
AND THE PEOPLE OF GOD

PAUL PEACHEY, Editor

FORTRESS PRESS   PHILADELPHIA

Library of Congress Cataloging-in-Publication Data

Main entry under title:
   Peace, politics, and the people of God.

      1. Peace—Religious aspects—Christianity—Addresses,
essays, lectures. 2. War—Religious aspects—
Christianity—Addresses, essays, lectures. 3. Pacifism
—Religious aspects—Christianity—Addresses, essays,
lectures. 4. Just war doctrine—Addresses, essays,
lectures. I. Peachey, Paul, 1918-
BT736.4.P449 1986   241'.6242   85-45490
ISBN 0-8006-1898-X

1831K85   Printed in the United States of America   1-1898

CONTENTS

CONTENTS

ACKNOWLEDGMENTS

Permission to reprint is gratefully acknowledged: The chapter by John H. Yoder, which appeared in altered form, is reprinted with permission from his *The Priestly Kingdom*, University of Notre Dame Press (1985). From James F. Childress and from the *Journal of Religious Ethics* 11/1 (Spring 1984) for his chapter, "Moral Discourse About War in the Early Church." The Charles P. Lutz chapter, "Objection to Participation in Combat: Legality and Morality," first appeared, in altered form, in *Academy: Lutherans in Profession*, vol. 38, nos. 3 and 4 (1982). Donald E. Miller, "A Biblical Approach to Human Rights" originally appeared as part of "Toward an Ecumenical Theology for Grounding Human Rights" in *Soundings*, vol. 67 (Summer 1984).

The editor is indebted to the Swarthmore College Peace Collection for access to the A. J. Muste Papers for his chapter, "Minorities with a Mission in the Churches."

Thanks are also due to the members of the War-Nation-Church Study Group, both to those who contributed papers to this volume, and to those who supported this venture in other ways. A special word of thanks goes to John Oliver Nelson, former chairman of the Church Peace Mission and long-time chairman of the Study Group, for editorial advice and support.

P.P.

INTRODUCTION

Catholic teaching begins in every case with a presumption against war and for peaceful settlement of disputes. In exceptional cases, determined by the moral principles of the just-war tradition, some uses of force are permitted.

The Challenge of Peace, iii

Since World War II an almost unnoticed revolution has occurred in the churches' teaching on church and war: the early Christian peace tradition has been readmitted into the forum of Christian thought and action. Virtually since the fourth century the pacifist witness in the churches of the West had been at best tolerated, at worst suppressed. But the two great conciliar events of the twentieth century, the establishment of the World Council of Churches (1948) and the Vatican II Council of the Roman Catholic Church (1965), both reembraced pacifism (and conscientious objection) as a valid and legitimate Christian option alongside the still dominant just-war doctrine.*

Something more sweeping was at stake, however, than tolerance for a minority view and practice within the churches. As the quotation above signifies, a rehabilitation of the original Christian "presumption against war and for the peaceful settlement of disputes" occurred. Indeed, the historical hypothesis that it was the eclipse of that presumption over the centuries which had led to the suppression of conscientious objection in the churches in the first place may be warranted.

Genuine revolutions seldom reveal their full consequences immediately. The present instance is no exception. As an issue, conscientious objection

---

Over the centuries, a doctrine was forged in Western Christianity which held that though war is an evil to be avoided, under given circumstances and controls it may be the lesser of evils, and, in that limited sense, "just."

1

directly affects a small number of persons, and only when universal military service is in force. But a recovery of the presumption against war and for the peaceful settlement of disputes, if taken seriously, will profoundly transform the whole Christian community. Can this happen? If so, how will it come to pass? What may we anticipate?

No prediction will be hazarded here. Obviously it will take more than mere statements by hierarchies and councils, or their elaboration by ethicists. Nonetheless, elaboration there must be, and in an unprecedented manner the task calls for the shared labor of "nonpacifist" and "pacifist" scholars. The present papers are offered in response to this task. They emerge from an off-the-record ecumenical (Protestant and Roman Catholic) conversation between nonpacifist and pacifist scholars that has been in progress for twenty years (see chap. 2).

These presentations are self-contained, and each can be read independently. Taken together, however, they constitute a larger whole. This is evident, on one level, in the sequence in which they appear. Part I sketches some of the recent pioneering for peace in the churches, along with some failures; part II presents some new and newly stated positions appearing in the churches today; and part III examines two current issues as case studies.

On another level these essays are organized around the seemingly perennial polarity of *Kirche* (the inclusive established church) and *Sekte* (the voluntary free church) as modes of Christian association. Church doctrines or polities and ethics are distinct categories, yet they tend to co-vary. Each church mode implies a corresponding ethic while each ethical mode presupposes a corresponding ecclesiology. This polarity energizes the three ecclesiological essays, those by Hehir, West, and Yoder. The nuclear era effectively forces each ecclesiology, the established church and the free church mode, in the direction of the other. In reaching for prophetic disengagement and witness, the established church may move toward sectarian withdrawal. In reaching for relevant witness the free church may dilute its own witness. These types, admittedly, are no longer—and may never have been—pure. In any event, the ecclesiological essays by Hehir, West, and Yoder play some new variations on these ancient themes.

The two case studies, conscientious objection and human rights, hold their own attraction. The former term, "conscientious objection," though well-entrenched, may be a misnomer. The exercise of conscience entails discernment and moral judgment. The religious pacifist, on the other hand, feels bound by a norm whose demand is absolute, and in that sense does not make a relative judgment. The "selective" objector of whom

Lutz writes, on the other hand, exercises moral judgment, and in this sense may properly be described as an objector of conscience. Ironically, however, for the U.S. Congress, it is precisely the selective objector who is problematic, and whose claim it has been least willing to recognize. Admittedly the notion is fraught with peril. In any event, the willingness of modern societies to accommodate pacifist objectors represents an extraordinary, if still precarious achievement.

Human rights, to take the second concern, and peace represent separate agendas in the political arena. Both practically and theologically, however, they are closely linked. Both are profound biblical themes, yet neither translates directly or readily into political programs. Donald Miller, in the next-to-last chapter in the volume, attributes contemporary concepts of human rights to the modern political experience. As crystallization of that experience, human-rights language thus does not appear directly in the Bible. Accordingly there is a danger that religious reflection content itself merely with efforts to fit itself to existing secular concepts.

Yet there are serious differences between the two conceptions. Contemporary secular conceptions of human rights frequently are torn from the fabric of mutuality and accountability into which rights are woven in the biblical vision of shalom. Beyond this, there are problems in the biblical materials as well. One of the more serious of these arises around the contrapuntal themes of nature and grace, themes that often resound dissonantly in theological recital. After several decades of "God acts in history" theology, Miller follows Brueggeman in reaccenting notes from the doctrine of creation, by extension, the "deontological" perspective in ethics. In no case will theology capture the public discourse on peace and human rights, nor is that an appropriate goal. As Miller implies, we have a different task, namely the rearticulation of an authentic witness.

John Oliver Nelson, a veteran Christian pacifist, and a participant in many of the events referenced in this volume, completes our journey with some questions designed to prompt discussion. But no attempt is made to close the circle limned by these writers. They are material for the revolution, only begun, that must transform the entire life and witness of the churches.

PAUL PEACHEY   Washington, D.C.
                                               February 1985

I

RECENT PIONEERING
IN PEACE

1

FROM HAUNTED SLEEP
TO A NEW AWAKENING: THE CHURCHES
AND DISARMAMENT IN AMERICA

ALAN GEYER

One of the most difficult, and most necessary, exercises in Christian scholarship is the interpretation of our most recent history. This exercise is particularly difficult—and all the more necessary—in matters of war and peace, defense and disarmament. For it is in these matters that national blinders, propaganda, censorship, and academic captivity are most likely to distort the past and prejudice the future.

Christianity as a transnational community has an extraordinary potential for transcending these mental barriers. Yet it cannot be said that theological scholarship has concocted adequate disciplines for interpreting recent world history, either ecclesiastical or political. There is a borderland between modern church history and political ethics that has yet to be substantially explored. Somehow, between the detachment we seek for studies of remoter periods and the topicality of our immediate concerns, we tend to shy away from systematic and critical analysis of what happened five or ten or twenty years ago. Perhaps this is partly because we want to slough off the wearisome burdens of our own yesterdays and make a fresh start on today's agenda. But the teaching of history in our educational systems at all levels tends to expire at the threshold of our own generation.

Our future study and action, however, are considerably determined by our past study and action—and neglect. It is our very bad habit as Americans and as "now, now, now!" Christians to plunge into every international

Dr. Alan Geyer is executive director of the Churches' Center for Theology and Public Policy in Washington, D.C. A political scientist and ethicist, he formerly served as editor of *The Christian Century* and Dag Hammarskjöld Professor of Peace Studies at Colgate University. He is the author of the 1982 book *The Idea of Disarmament: Rethinking the Unthinkable* (Elgin, Ill.: Brethren Press).

7

crisis as if it had no history. It is a habit which leads us to exaggerate our own innocence (in Indochina, Iran, Cuba, Central America, the development of MIRVs [multiple independently targeted reentry vehicle], the new nuclear arms race in Europe) and, therefore, to misunderstand the choices set before us. History, rightly understood, is not an excuse for regression and escape to the past: it is the unfolding of a dynamic pattern of action that we must perceive with some clarity if we are really serious about changing our institutions and policies.

The glib recounting of what happened in the 1960s was a preoccupation of many religious and political leaders throughout the 1970s and on into the 1980s—but that recounting was typically flawed by the most dubious mythological notions. Among the most misleading myths of recent history appropriate to this study are the following:

1. The churches were overextended in political action for justice and peace in the 1960s and, therefore, had to turn inward in retreat during the 1970s.

2. The social programs of the Great Society were mostly failures, thus proving that the federal government should sharply curtail its responsibilities for the general welfare, minorities, and the poor.

3. The American nation has been plagued for the last decade by a "Vietnam syndrome" that has crippled our will to world power, slackened our defenses to the point of virtual unilateral disarmament, and permitted the Soviets to gain strategic superiority and to make dramatic geopolitical progress toward world domination.

4. The basic theological and ethical issues of the nuclear age were adequately treated in the 1950s and early 1960s, requiring only some updating in details.

These widely held myths are not only based on misperceptions of the recent past, but they endure as perverse points of departure for future mission and policy. This chapter is, in part, an effort to demythologize such readings of our recent history.

The arms race is badly out of control. Massive new movements for disarmament have shaken the political foundations of Europe. There is a mounting confrontation in the United States between the regressive militarism of the Reagan administration and an array of resurgent disarmament activity unseen since the early 1960s. And the Soviet military buildups—in conventional forces, Euromissiles, bombers, and heavy strategic missiles—proceed without constraint. The Geneva arms-control negotiations on a Comprehensive Test Ban, on strategic arms (START), and on Euromissiles (INF) had all broken down by the end of 1983. Yet, both superpowers continued to profess their own commitment to arms reduction and to blame the adversary for the arms race. Cynicism about the true intentions of both became increasingly widespread, not only in the U.S., but throughout the world. What Alva Myrdal has called "the game of disarmament" once again seemed to be raising and manipulating false hopes. Yet, cynicism is never an adequate Christian response to political developments, particularly when the survival of the human species is at stake.

If the churches of America have recently been somewhat stirred by the new disarmament movements in both Europe and the U.S., the main burden of this account is to acknowledge that the mainline churches were mostly disengaged from defense and disarmament policy for fifteen years, from 1963 to 1978. There are several ways of telling this story. One is to look at the programs and priorities of denominational and ecumenical organizations in those years and to recognize how trivially those issues were treated. A second is to focus on decisive moments in U.S. policy making and inquire whether the churches had any role to play. A third is to provide a more theological account by asking what preoccupations and trends among the churches' leading thinkers may have contributed to the peripheral status of disarmament and peacemaking.

In the spring of 1980, the National Council of Churches held a major consultation on disarmament in Pittsburgh. One of the platform presentations was a survey by the NCC assistant general secretary, Peggy L. Shriver, of denominational and ecumenical pronouncements on disarmament during the previous decade. These pronouncements, taken together, were impressive in their sheer number, variety, prophetic urgency, and even theological richness. If our account ended there, we might conclude that the churches had indeed made disarmament just about the highest mission priority.

It is when we look candidly at what Dietrich Bonhoeffer called "the empirical reality of the church" that we are driven to a very different conclusion. Virtually none of those pronouncements from the mid-1960s to the late 1970s established any programs of continuing action on the issues of defense and disarmament. In fact, the NCC bureaucracy itself blocked every effort to designate even one full-time staff person to work on these issues. A very limited international affairs staff did provide, on a marginal basis, a remarkable amount of energy and activity to ecumenical and coalition groups in disarmament in the late 1970s. Of course, the NCC itself tended to reflect the priorities and pressures of its member communions, and none of the mainline Protestant denominations provided as much as a single staff person to work full-time on defense and disarmament issues during these same years.

Both preoccupation with the Vietnam War and subsequent retreat from the activism of the 1960s help to explain this pattern of neglect. The decade of the 1970s turned out to be the most regressive era in the American churches since the 1920s. That fact is inextricably tangled up in the larger political environment of a decade which experienced four essentially conservative presidents: Nixon, Ford, Carter, Reagan. While there were some liberal impulses in the early months of the Carter administration, the churches did very little to reinforce them. All through the 1970s, many church leaders provided excuses for privatized religion, institutional "consolidation," and new "church growth" strategies at the expense of the struggle for justice and peace. In the process, much of the history of the 1960s—both religious and political—was misrepresented and mythologized. Religious narcissism was in; prophetic engagement was out.

These institutional defaults were reflected in theological education, where very few seminaries defined disarmament and peacemaking as central tasks of professional ministry; in church-related higher education, where only a handful of colleges had developed a serious curriculum in defense and disarmament studies (even new peace-studies programs typically slighted these issues); in the churches' print and broadcast media, where these issues were only sporadically and superficially touched upon; and in missions and international affairs programs of denominations and ecumenical councils, which never made the understanding of U.S.-Soviet relations an educational imperative. The parochial history of the churches' international education has been largely captive to the geography of missionary enterprises—China, India, southern Africa, Latin America. Without discounting the importance of those areas, the neglect of the Soviet Union, even of Soviet churches, is one of the most serious shortcomings of the U.S. churches throughout three decades of cold war.

So it is not simply the slighting of strategic and technical questions related to the arms race that must be recounted: it is the lack of sustained professional attention to Soviet history, culture, politics, and church life—which provide the human context for disarmament—that must be acknowledged. The ad hoc exchanges and consultations of the past several years—notably the "Choose Life" consultations—have proved to be extremely significant events in U.S.-Soviet ecumenism. But they are no substitute for ongoing programs of education and encounter that reach out to the churches' congregational constituency. Perhaps the best hope, ultimately, for defusing weapons of mass annihilation is the multiplication of education and exchange programs that humanize the "enemy."

The consequences of religious disengagement from disarmament in the 1960s and 1970s may be brought into sharper focus if we recount the most crucial decisional moments in the arms race in those same years. Our context for future action is much shaped by past action—and by past inaction. In this sketchy recollection of the arms race, we shall skip over the wartime decisions to develop and to drop atomic bombs—decisions inaccessible to the public then and irremediable now and forever: the ill-fated 1946 proposal for international control of atomic energy; the H-bomb decision of 1949; the largely unchallenged doctrine of massive retaliation in the early 1950s; and the missile race of the early 1960s. Yet, in all these matters except the first, there was an opening for effective Christian testimony that was largely neglected.

ACDA AND THE TEST BAN

There was some significant church advocacy for the establishment of the new U.S. Arms Control and Disarmament Agency in 1961 and for the Limited Test Ban of 1963. Those efforts were not, however, steadfastly followed up in subsequent years with the mobilization of a constituency for the new agency or for the completion of a Comprehensive Test Ban. ACDA remains a mini-agency with a mini-budget and a mini-staff, too frequently overpowered, if not bypassed, by the Pentagon, the CIA, and the National Security staff at the White House. The key arms-control appointees in the Reagan administration, ACDA director Eugene Rostow and strategic negotiators General Edward Rowny and Paul Nitze were all hardline anti-Soviet men who joined in leading the opposition to SALT II (Strategic Arms Limitation Talks).

There has been much more nuclear testing—albeit underground testing—since 1963 than there was before the test ban. Neither the technical nor diplomatic obstacles to a Comprehensive Test Ban have been as great as the domestic political and bureaucratic obstacles which even now cannot be overcome without constituency pressure—which the churches could rally if they willed to do so. Yet, the churches have been inconstant in their support for an end to all nuclear testing. There is, perhaps, no step on the long road to nuclear disarmament that could prove to be more vital than the completion, at long, long last, of a Comprehensive Test Ban. It is an unfulfilled commitment under the Nuclear Non-Proliferation Treaty of 1968 which could do much to restore the cooperative will required to halt the further spread of nuclear weapons. But a test ban is also a very practical earnest of our determination to halt the further escalation of military technology, which has long since reached a level of extreme dissociation from the world's real human problems.

11

ABMs AND MIRVs

The years 1965 to 1972 were years of massive U.S. involvement in Indochina, conspicuous religious opposition to the war, bitter struggles over the draft and the rights of selective objectors, and severe social and political turmoil on the home front. But neither the churches nor the general public was aware then, nor do they remember now, that that same period was punctuated by U.S. decisions to forge ahead with new generations of both defensive and offensive nuclear weapons. It is precisely those decisions that now haunt the frustrating quest for strategic arms limitation in the 1980s, especially decisions about the development and deployment of MIRVs. National organizations like SANE (Committee for a Sane Nuclear Policy) which, with substantial religious participation, had campaigned for a nuclear test ban in the early 1960s became absorbed in the antiwar movement and largely abandoned disarmament and related nuclear issues.

In December 1965, the White House Conference on International Cooperation proposed a moratorium on the development of anti-ballistic missiles (ABMs). The rationale for the proposed moratorium is important to remember. That proposal, framed by an arms-control panel chaired by Jerome Wiesner of MIT, former science adviser to President Kennedy, was based on the paradoxical judgment that "defensive" missiles could be dangerously provocative: they would probably provoke the development of new hydra-headed offensive missiles, or MIRVs. The pattern of the arms race was clear: offensive technology would forever outstrip defensive technology, though the latter could catalyze the former. There could be no effective defense against nuclear weapons. Therefore, the wisest course would be to prevent further stimuli to offensive technologies.

It was an open moment: a precious opportunity to appeal to reason in lifting ourselves above the fatalistic scenarios of weapons designers. It was the perception of that opportunity which helped anticipate what the SALT talks could have become.

Many church groups were represented at that White House conference. But, apart from a few mailings from the historic peace churches and resolutions in two or three mainline bodies, there was no significant Christian action on the ABM issue for the next twenty-one months. There was no mobilized constituency in the general public.

Both the U.S. and USSR proceeded with their provocative ABM programs, soon to be followed by MIRVs. It came as a great shock to the arms-control community that Secretary of Defense Robert McNamara, who had himself publicly and privately argued against ABMs, was obliged by Presi-

12

dent Johnson to announce in San Francisco on September 18, 1967, that the U.S. was going ahead with an ABM system after all. An essentially anti-Chinese rationale was offered. Yet, the whole logic of the McNamara speech seemed to argue against any new "generation" of weapons: the superpowers, he warned, must break free of "the mad momentum" generated by the "action-reaction phenomenon" that could lead them both to annihilation.

That ABM decision was made without a public policy debate, without effective church resistance, and with scant regard to its international political implications. Moreover, having grossly exaggerated the ABM technology of the Russians, the U.S. pushed ahead with its own MIRV development in the late 1960s—and finally to the deployment of MIRVs on both our land-based (ICBMs, intercontinental ballistic missiles) and submarine-based (SLBMs, sea-launched ballistic missiles) weapons in 1970.

Curiously, the U.S. and USSR were willing to agree on a treaty in 1972, the ABM Treaty, which officially recognized, at last, that anti-missile technology could not provide any viable defense against nuclear war. But by then the MIRV age had been inaugurated. The rationale for MIRVs had been thoroughly undone. But the folly of forging ahead, now widely acknowledged, met little public resistance even though there was substantial congressional opposition in 1970 and 1971. This was one of those occasions not always perceived by church leaders when Congress was well in advance of the public, but needed effective constituency support in order to prevail against the Pentagon. But the churches were silent on the MIRV issue. And the United States, by the end of the 1970s, had four times as many strategic nuclear warheads—that is, separately targetable missile warheads—as it had at the beginning of the decade. Contrary to alarmist mythology, the U.S. was hardly standing still, and certainly not unilaterally disarming, all during the last decade.

Of course, the Soviets did not stand still either. They caught on to the MIRV technology four or five years after the U.S. did. By 1980, they had acquired twice as many separately targetable missile warheads as they had in 1970. It is precisely the MIRVing of their heavy missiles that made the right-wing opponents of SALT, like Paul Nitze (who were once among the chief promoters of U.S. MIRVs), so alarmist about the threat of a Soviet first strike: the incredible fantasy of the "window of vulnerability." If the U.S. does not ratify the SALT II Treaty which limits heavy ICBMs to ten warheads, each one of those Soviet missiles could mount thirty or perhaps even forty warheads. The Reagan administration provided the bizarre

13

spectacle of arms-control officials (Rostow, Rowny, Nitze) who opposed a treaty favored by the Joint Chiefs of Staff.

FROM DETERRENCE TO COUNTERFORCE

Since 1970, while MIRVs have been multiplying the warheads, the strategic debate has shifted once again. It has shifted from the deterrence of nuclear war with retaliatory second-strike weapons to the morally deceptive doctrines of counterforce. It may well be that there has always been some sub rosa notion of counterforce: of a relentless drive toward nuclear superiority by threatening to wipe out the Soviets' own deterrent forces. But the doctrines of mutual assured destruction (MAD) have been increasingly displaced since 1970 by the doctrines of nuclear-war fighting, limited nuclear war, the fantasies of nuclear-war winning, and the implicit threat of a nuclear first strike.

Counterforce dogma is rationalized as more moral because military forces, not cities, are said to be the prime targets. The technological reality behind that claim is that most of the new weapons are not only more accurate, they are more devastating and will just as surely annihilate tens of millions of people in any credible attack. Moreover, the dogma that counterforce weapons are more "usable" because they are more accurate and more "moral" severely weakens whatever inhibitions remain against any resort to nuclear weapons. And, because counterforce dogma carries with it that implicit threat of a first strike, it has surely raised pressures upon the Soviet military establishment to build up its own first-strike capacity, if not actually to contemplate seriously a preemptive attack against the U.S.

It is counterforce dogma that has provided the intellectual dynamic for pushing ahead with Trident missiles and subs, Mark 12-A warheads, MX missiles, air-launched cruise missiles, and that new pair of theater missiles for NATO approved on December 12, 1979: ground-launched cruise missiles (GLCMs) and Pershing II rockets, both capable of devastating the Soviet Union from close range. It is deployment of these new NATO weapons, beginning in December 1983, which has made nuclear war a renewed backyard issue for Europeans and provoked the launching of the new mass movements for disarmament. While this NATO "modernization" program was rationalized as a response to Soviet SS-20s, NATO already had thousands of nuclear weapons in the European region. Yet it must be said that the U.S. churches were hardly aroused on this issue in 1979 and have yet to gauge the depth and breadth of European concern, nor have they effectively challenged the crude stereotypes of Europeans purveyed by the administration and some journalists. Some groups like the American Friends Service Committee and Clergy and Laity Concerned (CALC) did attempt to publicize the NATO issue in 1979 and have since promoted exchanges with leaders of the European movements.

Whatever the churches may do to oppose any of these particular weapon systems, they must confront the mass of doctrine that is rationalizing, if not propelling, the next great leap forward in the nuclear arms race. Political effectiveness in this arena of public policy requires a capacity to cope with strategic arguments and their implications for disarmament.

Those who led the campaign against the B-1 bomber early in the Carter administration, largely on the grounds of its costliness, did not understand clearly enough that the trade-off, cruise missiles, was much more upsetting to U.S.-Soviet relations and infinitely more threatening to the prospects for effective arms control. Yet, now the B-1 is being resurrected, after all—only to be followed by still another new bomber, the "Stealth."

When President Nixon first revealed a serious inclination toward counterforce in 1970, when he named counterforce protagonist Fred Ikle ACDA director in 1973, when Secretary of Defense Harold Brown surfaced as a counterforce advocate in 1979, when Jimmy Carter disclosed his Presidential Directive 59 for a "countervailing strategy" in August 1980—on all these occasions church leadership was poorly prepared to conduct a vital moral debate on the implications of counterforce for detente and disarmament.

NON-PROLIFERATION

The combined impact of MIRV technology, counterforce doctrine, and the Soviets' persistent catch-ups—all since 1970—has been to undermine the fragile patchwork of disarmament agreements and processes that emerged during the 1960s.

The Non-Proliferation Treaty (NPT), which took effect in 1970, has been grossly vitiated by both superpowers. That treaty's pledge of a Comprehensive Test Ban and its "good faith" Article VI (which promised nuclear arms reductions) provided the solemn covenant which induced 116 nations to renounce nuclear weapons for themselves. Had the churches been significantly involved in the preparatory work for, and the actual deliberations of, the first Non-Proliferation Review Conference in Geneva in 1975, the moral seriousness of that covenant might have been much better understood by the American public in the mid-1970s. Instead, the public never knew the conference was even taking place, even though it was at that time the largest and most significant disarmament conference since World War II.

Nor was much of the American public aware that the second NPT Review Conference occurred in August 1980 and that it witnessed the virtual breakdown of cooperative efforts to halt the spread of nuclear weapons. Continuing defaults on a test ban and SALT II were largely to blame. The conference adjourned in exasperation, disarray, and mutual recrimination. While several church representatives were present and contributed to NGO (nongovernmental organizations) activities, including the unofficial conference newspaper *Disarmament Times*, church constituencies were hardly engaged in any significant way.

SALT

The SALT talks, which got under way in November 1969, never seriously confronted the very challenge they were designed to forestall: the new generation of offensive weapons technology represented by MIRVs. By the time of the SALT I accords in 1972, U.S. MIRVs had already been deployed. Even Henry Kissinger later lamented his own failure to think through the implications of MIRV technology for the arms race. How much more determined should the churches in the early 1970s have been to make the SALT talks an auspicious opportunity to reverse the arms race instead of a license to escalate it?

The SALT II Treaty (1979), whose substantive provisions are obscurely technical and frustratingly modest, offered a potential turning point in the arms race because it established a framework for negotiating substantial reductions. Symbolically and politically, it was "the centerpiece of detente," as U.S. and Soviet leaders repeatedly said. Church representatives, organized in a coalition through the Religious Committee on SALT, lobbied intensively for the treaty's ratification. Most denominations, however, failed to provide the financial or constituency support required to make the lobby truly effective. Indeed, pro-SALT senators complained candidly that they received little grass-roots support from the churches. The campaign's work was also complicated by opposition to the treaty from some pacifist and radical Christians on the left. The Carter administration's delays and retreats on SALT II, which virtually killed the treaty by the fall of 1979, were then rationalized by the Soviet Union's attack on Afghanistan in late December. With the demise of SALT II and the election of an anti-SALT president in 1980, the nuclear arms race rocketed out of control, more so than at any time in two decades.

THE UNITED NATIONS

Paralleling the bilateral diplomacy of the SALT process, a new pattern of multilateral diplomacy and global bargaining on disarmament (and other issues) emerged during the 1970s. The two review conferences on the Non-Proliferation Treaty and an array of United Nations activities provided the most significant expressions of this pattern. At the heart of the new multilateral diplomacy was an escalating moral conflict between the world's nuclear haves and nuclear have-nots.

In the spring of 1978, the United Nations convened its first Special Session on Disarmament: an unprecedented opportunity for the United States to help forge a new multilateral consensus. Thanks to thorough preparation by many other governments, the presence of twenty-three heads of state or government, and the vital contributions of some NGOs (non-governmental organizations), that Special Session significantly upgraded UN machinery for disarmament and generated a welcome variety of new policy proposals. But the boycott of that Assembly by President Carter, the lack of any substantial policy initiatives from the administration, the short shrift given the Assembly by the media, and the meager engagement of the churches made the Special Session a nonevent for the American public. Largely because of the Reagan administration's disdain for the UN and its aggressive "rearmament" program, the Second UN Special Session on Disarmament in 1982 broke down in a political stalemate. Owing partly to the more active involvement of church leaders this time, however, the 1982 session was the occasion for the largest peace rally in American history when a million marchers converged on Central Park to join in massive support for nuclear disarmament. If the rally itself was a potent boost to the Nuclear Freeze, NGO activities in and around the Special Session helped to solidify the links of an emerging multinational disarmament movement, especially among Europeans and North Americans.

The basic problems of disarmament are political and moral. They are problems of persuading millions of people that all strategic and technical issues must be contained within a framework of humane understanding and moral choice. They are problems of mustering the courage to refuse to surrender the choice of life for ourselves and our children to either the hate-mongers or the anonymous bureaucratic momentum of military technology. They are problems of doctrine: how to bring the transcendent doctrines of our faith to bear upon those idolatrous doctrines that rationalize every new weapon of mass destruction which perverse ingenuity can imagine, even while blaming other nations for the stupidity of it all. And

17

they are problems of the human ego: how to be spiritually strong enough to plunge into this struggle for human survival—and to stay in this struggle for years and years to come—without that messianic arrogance so rife in the peace movement itself and so costly to the practical political possibilities of a more-or-less democratic society.

DISARMAMENT AND THE THEOLOGIANS

Whatever the defaults of governmental and ecclesiastical institutions in restraining the arms race, what can be said about the American churches' principal theologians in the period from 1963 to 1978? To what extent were they centrally involved in the intellectual and moral struggles over the most critical issues of security and disarmament?

In the late 1950s and early 1960s, theologians had indeed been centrally involved in such struggles. Reinhold Niebuhr, John Bennett, Paul Ramsey, and a host of younger theologians and ethicists grappled with nuclear deterrence, counterforce, just-war doctrines, the morality of The Bomb, and the ideological confrontations of the cold war. Whatever the adequacy of their work, then or now, the churches' most eminent theologians in the first nuclear generation felt called upon to address the issues of national security (if not disarmament).

Since the early 1960s, the same quality of theological engagement has been all too rare. The preoccupations of ethicists since the mid-1960s have been largely with bioethics, sexuality, technology, language, and methodology. Black and liberation theologians since the late 1960s have been understandably preoccupied with the maximization of power and their agendas of justice—but only marginally with the arms race and peacemaking. Indeed, they have tended to criticize the new anti-nuclear movements of the 1980s as being captive to white middle-class interests. The relationship of peace with justice, both theologically and politically, has emerged as a painful issue for U.S. churches and for the World Council of Churches in the past several years.

The most significant theological work in peacemaking in the early 1980s was less that of academic theologians and more that of denominational and ecumenical circles: the Presbyterians' *Peacemaking: The Believer's Calling*, the historic peace churches' *New Call to Peacemaking*, the Pastoral Letter of the U.S. Catholic Bishops, *The Challenge of Peace: God's Promise and Our Response*, and, internationally, the World Council of Churches' report of its 1981 Amsterdam Nuclear Hearing titled *Before It's Too Late*, and the 1983 Vancouver Assembly documents—to mention a few of the most significant works. The Catholic Bishops were notably candid in acknowledging the unmet need for theological reconstruction:

> This pastoral letter is more an invitation to continue the new appraisal of war and peace than a final synthesis of such an appraisal. We have a sense of the characteristics of a theology of peace, but not a systematic statement of their relationships.

This pattern of theological disengagement from 1963 to 1980 would be more bearable if those issues took the same shape in the 1980s that they assumed in the 1950s. The reality is dramatically different. Among the issues that now cry out for fresh theological work are the following:

1. *Nuclear equity.* The power of nuclear-weapon states to annihilate each other is also the power to destroy still other nations. Radioactive fallout and ozone depletion from a major nuclear war could devastate a country with no belligerent status at all. The severity of such injustices is especially acute for the 116 nations that have renounced nuclear weapons under the Non-Proliferation Treaty in return for a legal commitment to nuclear disarmament by nuclear-weapon states. The demoralizing effect of the nuclear arms race is compounded by the increase in nuclear-weapon and nuclear-prone states. Thus, the very meaning of nationhood, sovereignty, and self-determination has been vitiated by these threats to survival. What, after all, are the legitimate rights of nations in the face of nuclear imperialism and absolutism?

2. *The autonomy of military technology.* Both democratic and authoritarian political systems appear to be increasingly under the sway of an uncontrolled bureaucratic momentum in military technology. Habitual cycles of weapons research, development, production, and deployment proceed with diminishing political guidance and accountability—and even with diminishing reference to adversary weapons systems. Have the institutional drives of military technology become incompatible with democratic politics and a rational foreign policy? Shall the churches regard such a weapons culture as belonging to demonic principalities and powers that must be categorically rejected?

3. *National defense and social justice.* Have the costs of military policies—now over half of all federal operating costs in the U.S.—become so exorbitant that they undermine the very values those policies are supposed to defend? Is the effective power of government crippled by diminishing economic strength and forfeiting the general welfare of the people? What groups in society become increasingly defenseless in the name of "defense"? Who really pays the costs of the military establishment: the

rich or the poor? How many social programs must be "sacrificed" for military budgets—and who suffers most from such sacrifices?

4. *Disarmament and development.* With world military expenditures of $1 trillion a year—that is $1 billion every nine hours—the relationship between the arms race and world poverty is more critical than ever. The 1980 report of the Brandt Commission on International Development noted the following item of human scale: one-half of one percent of one year's world military expenditure would pay for all the farm equipment needed to increase food production to the level of self-sufficiency in the world's food-deficit countries by 1990. Is this datum—this earthy connection between the arms race and hunger—not worthy of the most fundamental theological imperatives? Is ours not a faith that requires the beating of bombers into plowshares and missiles into pruning hooks?

5. *Initiative and responsibility.* The failure of the superpowers to contain their own arms race raises the question as to whether they have reached a bilateral deadlock from which neither seems capable of breaking free. Yet, each government continues to make unilateral decisions to escalate the arms race with new weapons systems. Do nuclear "powers" retain any political power to transform the system of mutual terror? Does either superpower have a special responsibility to take independent action to unwind the spiral? What is the theological basis of unilateral initiatives? How much is reciprocity a condition of initiatives? Does "parity" merit any special theological or ethical significance?

6. *National security and transnational imperatives.* In a "world community of risk," national security can hardly remain a matter of going it alone. How shall we understand security biblically, theologically, and ethically in such a world? Is security basically a matter of *realpolitik*—or is it part of God's promise of liberation? Is it not indivisible from justice and peace?

7. *The church as a multinational fellowship.* The insecurities, fears, hostilities, and injustices experienced by any nation must be understood by other nations if peacemaking is to lead to a stable and secure world community. The church is a unique fellowship for the sharing of diverse national traumas and hopes. There can hardly be a more ultimate meaning of ecumenism than this actual experience of human diversity and solidarity across all boundaries, especially in matters of survival of the species. What is the place of multinational missions in the work of disarmament and peacemaking? How can Americans be led to understand their own need of missions from European, Third World, and "enemy" countries?

There is a startling discovery yet to be made by most theologians who have concerned themselves with the traditional debates among pacifists, just-war theorists, and "Christian realists": those distinctions are preoccupied with alternative orientations to war itself. They have to do with whether, when, or how to support war as a national policy—or to participate in war as a matter of individual choice. They do not, however, qualify as fully developed theologies of war *and peace*. This preoccupation with typologies of Christian attitudes toward war has tended to prevent the emergence of *typologies of peacemaking* among both pacifists and nonpacifists. Disarmament, as an essential element of peacemaking, has therefore been a victim of the most serious theological neglect.

As suggested earlier, much theological work is yet to be done by way of demythologizing strategic dogmas like nuclear deterrence and counterforce which received much attention a generation ago in a very different world political situation. It is precisely the dogmatic character of rationalizations for the arms race that must be addressed anew. If the pacifist-nonpacifist debate has been overtaken by new forces of politics and technology, so has the deterrence-counterforce debate.

A fresh critique of deterrence (which I have attempted in my 1982 study, *The Idea of Disarmament: Rethinking the Unthinkable*) ought to emphasize the following perspectives, among others:

1. The incoherent and speculative character of much deterrence doctrine.

2. The tendency of deterrence to reinforce reactive and isolationist tendencies in foreign policy.

3. The technocratic and militaristic biases of deterrence theories which provide escapes from political wisdom and effective diplomacy.

4. The bilateral fixations of deterrence at a time of uncontrolled nuclear proliferation.

5. The negative preoccupation with threats to the neglect of positive inducements.

6. The contradictions between excessive confidence in nuclear rationality and subhuman images of enemies.

7. Deterrence is not simply a matter of ethical calculation: it has become a dogmatic rival to religious faith by putting its own ultimate faith in the power of fear.

The Catholic Bishops' Pastoral Letter in its second of four drafts contained a sharp repudiation of "the negative dimensions of deterrence." The final draft, however, deleted that five-point critique in favor of Pope John Paul II's statement presented to the 1982 UN Special Session that deterrence might be "a step toward progressive disarmament" and, therefore, could be judged "morally acceptable." Later in the UN Session, General Secretary Philip Potter of the World Council of Churches expressed a contrary view: Deterrence "can in no way be a step toward disarmament.

On the contrary, it has fueled, and continues to fuel the arms race at various levels. The concept of deterrence is, thus, politically unacceptable and morally indefensible." The WCC's Vancouver Assembly in 1983 adopted similar language in its policy statement on peace and justice.

In the U.S. churches, nuclear deterrence emerged in 1982 and 1983 as the new central issue for theological and ethical debate in matters of peacemaking.

Counterforce doctrines, ambiguously related to deterrence, tend to compound the faults of deterrence in escalating the nuclear arms race—and much more. The speciousness of moral claims for counterforce weapons, targeted on military and command sites, is exposed by the indiscriminate massiveness of counterforce devastation. Many strategic targets are located in or near the most populous areas. (One MX missile, with ten warheads, may have two hundred to three hundred times the power of the Hiroshima A-bomb.) The unfounded optimism about the usability of nuclear weapons, the rational control of a "limited nuclear war," and the new temptations to nuclear superiority (or "margin of safety") is overdue for rigorous theological criticism. The Catholic Bishops' Pastoral Letter at least expressed great skepticism about such concepts. The tendency of counterforce weapons to frustrate technologies of verification compounds the fear of adversaries and increases pressures to contemplate a preemptive strike. Mobile strategic missiles and ground- and sea-launched cruise missiles may yet defeat the practical possibility of disarmament agreements based on national technical means of verification.

THE NEW AWAKENING

The emphasis of this account so far has been on the practical and intellectual disengagement of U.S. mainline churches from disarmament and security issues for nearly two decades. But the scene has changed spectacularly in the early 1980s. We have earlier referred to the renewal of engagement since 1978 and some of the forms it has taken. Some of these recent stirrings bear mention here.

The National Council of Churches has held a series of bilateral dialogues on disarmament and security with churches of the USSR, East Germany, South Korea, China, and Japan. The U.S.-USSR "Choose Life" Consultation in Geneva in March 1979 produced the first joint theological statement ever between church leaders of the two superpowers. That statement was published in *Izvestia*, as well as many Christian journals in the West. It led to the Pittsburgh Disarmament Consultation of 1980, as well as to subsequent U.S.-USSR dialogues which seem to have become a regular feature of the ecumenical landscape. Another fruit of the "Choose Life" consultations came in 1983 when NBC television broadcast two one-hour documentaries on "The Church of the Russians," narrated by Bruce Rigdon of McCormick Seminary. The National Council of Churches has established a U.S.-USSR Church Relations Committee which in 1984 sponsored four exchange programs, two in each country.

The National Conference of Catholic Bishops' Pastoral Letter on War and Peace has provided one of the most dramatic church-state confrontations and educational processes in American experience. While the bishops finally offered a "strictly conditioned" legitimation of nuclear deterrence, they supported a nuclear freeze and a Comprehensive Test Ban, at the same time rejecting first-strike and nuclear-war fighting strategies. Their pastoral letter is rich in scriptural, historical, and pastoral resources for Christian education. Individual bishops have become increasingly vocal in their opposition to nuclear weapons.

Some Catholic orders, especially the Maryknoll community and the sisterhoods involved in common witness through NETWORK (a Catholic social justice lobby), have become vital ecumenical partners in political action for disarmament.

The World Conference on Religion and Peace, led by its U.S. secretary general, Homer Jack, has provided strong disarmament leadership for both religious and nonreligious groups in the United Nations community, especially in enlarging the opportunities for NGO participation since the UN Special Session on Disarmament in 1978.

Several denominations—notably the Presbyterian Church USA, the United Church of Christ, the United Methodist Church, the American Baptist Churches, and the American Lutheran Church—have recently instituted substantial study-action programs on peacemaking and disarmament. The leaders of some denominations have obviously been deeply affected by their participation in NCC dialogues with Soviet church leaders.

The historic peace churches—Quakers, Mennonites, Brethren—continue not only to empower their own small memberships, but to spur and equip the mainliners. Their recent "New Call to Peacemaking" is a vital ecumenical venture that has undergirded the repudiation of war with a positive theology and program for peace.

The Washington-based Sojourners Community and Evangelicals for Social Action inspired a new commitment to disarmament on the part of many "evangelicals"—including Billy Graham.

Riverside Church in New York and the Church of the Savior in Washington, D.C., while hardly typical local churches, have given extraordinary congregational leadership in the past three years in helping to forge local and regional links around the country.

Regional interfaith centers to mobilize public opposition to the arms race have been established in such places as Pasadena, California, and Princeton, New Jersey.

A religious task force of the Mobilization for Survival since 1978 has recruited church activists for mass action and civil disobedience on behalf of disarmament.

A Nuclear Freeze Campaign was launched in 1980 with the support of the National Council of Churches and a number of denominations, as well as nonchurch groups, and is committed to "a mutual freeze on the testing, production, and deployment of nuclear weapons and of missiles and new aircraft designed primarily to deliver nuclear weapons."

An intensive nationwide educational program on nuclear weapons called Ground Zero Week enlisted the support of the National Council of Churches, the Catholic bishops, and a number of denominations (along with labor unions, educational associations, and citizen action groups) for the week of April 18–25, 1982.

The ecumenical Churches' Center for Theology and Public Policy established disarmament as one of its four major research and program priorities at its inauguration in 1977. The Center has assisted many of the abovementioned organizations and efforts and has contributed substantially to the disarmament and militarism studies of the World Council of Churches.

Notwithstanding all these new stirrings, the military and arms-control policies of the United States in 1985 continue to escalate the nuclear arms race—as do those of the Soviet Union. While churches and theologians must be faithful even in the midst of their failures, they cannot be indifferent to the imperatives of successful disarmament and peacemaking. Unending failure in this Earth-threatening realm is an increasingly apocalyptic issue.

The main theme of the 1983 Assembly of the World Council of Churches in Vancouver—"Jesus Christ, the Life of the World"—must be absolutely affirmed with literal seriousness by congregations in every country and by all Christians together. For the very life of the world is indeed what disarmament is all about. Any doctrine or policy of defense or national security that is not based on such an ultimate pro-life vision for Planet Earth is, at best, an anachronism—and, at worst, the ultimate profanation of God's good creation.

2

MINORITIES
WITH A MISSION IN
THE CHURCHES

PAUL PEACHEY

The 1980s dawned under an increasingly ominous international sky. The sunshine of superpower detente was clouding over, and threats of nuclear war rumbled like distant thunder. If the clouds showed any possible silver lining, it was the rather abrupt awakening of public opinion, notably in the churches. Suddenly the public discovered that actual rather than mere deterrent use of nuclear weapons was under consideration. While the laity organized for public action, official church bodies in a number of countries were staking out unprecedented positions in opposition to nuclear weaponry. Mainline church leaders began to wonder audibly whether the time had come for their charges to declare themselves "peace churches."

If the stir in the churches was a hopeful sign, it was fraught, nonetheless, with uncertainty. Where can—or where should—a religiously inspired repudiation of nuclear weapons go? After all, skeptics may well observe, such an act leaves untouched the complex conflicts of which nuclear weapons are but the symptom. Moreover, peace movements in the past have mushroomed only to subside, slowly or quickly, because they were merely reactive phenomena. Spokesmen for the Reagan administration in the early months let it be known that they anticipated a similar fate for the then-current movement.

Peace movements owe their existence to war and related military actions, hardly possessing a life of their own. War, for its part, however, as suggested by the famous dictum of Karl von Clausewitz, is simply the continuation of diplomacy by other means. While wars usually begin in some trigger event, events that *trigger* do not *cause* wars. Wars grow from existing conflicts,

---

Paul Peachey, who served as executive secretary of the Church Peace Mission during the 1960s, currently teaches sociology at the Catholic University of America, Washington, D.C.

already possessing a life of their own. But how about peace movements? To what extent do they represent abiding commitments by their adherents to the peaceful resolution of conflict? To what extent are they merely reactive, without substance of their own? Are such movements ineffective for lack of root or substance, or are their demands simply unattainable?

On the surface, the anti-nuclear actions of the early 1980s appeared to differ little from peace movements of other days. Millions of people on both sides of the Atlantic were aroused by the continuing development and deployment of ever more destructive weapons, and by speculations by public officials over the winnability of nuclear war. The result was protests and marches. Most of the energies behind these actions, however, originated in the churches, a fact which suggested that something more than fear may have been at work. Many who are inspired by Christian faith and hope find the possession, the deployment, or the possible use of nuclear weapons to be an ultimate blasphemy.

But more is afoot in the churches than most people, both inside and outside, realize. It is not only that the nuclear threat, in the words of the hymn writer, makes ancient truths "uncouth." It is also that the rapid growth of global interdependence has poured new content into the ancient ecumenical vision. Suddenly the just-war ethic, long taken for granted in the churches, for the most part uncritically, is thrown into doubt, while the pacifist challenge, long ignored, once more gains a hearing.

The claim, of course, is not that the just-war doctrine has been abandoned or that the majority of Christians are about to become pacifists. It is to assert, rather, that in the flux of this era, many, perhaps most, people in the churches are driven to reexamine the foundations of both faith and ethics, and are discovering hitherto unfamiliar parts of the Christian legacy.

It was long the conventional view in Christian ethics that the pacifism of early Christians, though plausible in the first generations, became obsolete as Christianity moved from minority to majority status. Likewise, it was thought that the just-war doctrine embodied perennial principles or truth. Whether or not those assumptions were valid, the nuclear era reveals that the just-war doctrine, like the pacifism that preceded it, was in some measure the product of a particular historical era, but an era now passing.

The claim by some that nuclear weapons can in no way be justified by the just-war doctrine, or by others that such weapons render the doctrine itself obsolete, creates a novel situation. The just-war doctrine loses the monopoly it once held in the churches, and the common ground between the two conceptions, pacifism and the just war, suddenly appears broader than imagined earlier. That is, once the position is taken that certain actions are forbidden, even at the risk of defeat or occupation by an enemy, we have entered the pacifist "predicament." Once the use of nuclear weapons is rejected categorically, the question is no longer *whether* but, rather, *where* to draw the line.

To a degree unprecedented perhaps since the early centuries of the churches, pacifists and nonpacifists find themselves side by side in the churches, needing to take each other seriously. Few, if any, are prepared for this transformation. The nonpacifist option is likely to remain predominant in most parishes, with pacifists still an uncomfortable minority. But none can escape the sea change now upon us in the ethics of war and peace.

THE ECLIPSE OF CHRISTIAN PACIFISM

Historians report no evidence of Christians bearing arms prior to about A.D. 170. Arms-bearing by Christians became general only with the fourth-century establishment of Christianity as the imperial religion. Though taking human life, for whatever reason, was explicitly rejected by early Christian writers, historians do not agree on the reasons for early Christian refusals to bear arms. By the third century, objections to military service apparently had more to do with the conflict between Christian and Roman values generally, particularly the religious overtones of military oath, than with pacifism specifically. Whatever the facts, as Roland Bainton shows in a standard work on Christians and war, three major positions emerged in the history of the church: pacifism, the just-war doctrine, and the Crusade.[1] Though the Crusade notion remains as a perennial temptation, only the first two paradigms, the pacifist and the just war, can lay serious claim to the Christian conscience today.

At the outset of the Christian movement, however, there was little ambiguity. There was no place for bloodshed and war in the new reality embodied in the presence of Jesus, in his passion and resurrection, and in the Pentecost event. As the early accounts show, the impulses of love and community building were overwhelming. People were drawn together in the simultaneous discovery of personhood and the community. Their whole historical existence was transformed by the new order which had erupted in their midst, and which led them to anticipate an imminent Parousia. The resulting faith paradigm was summed up eloquently by a participant: "Christ also suffered for you, leaving you an example, that you should follow in his steps. . . . When he was reviled, he did not revile in return; when he suffered, he did not threaten; but he trusted to him who judges justly."[2]

It must be recognized, nonetheless, that the "pacifism" of the early

Christian bands was, in part, a function of historical circumstances. Apart from the temptation offered by the Zealot resistance "movement," to which two or more of the twelve apostles originally belonged, military action of whatever sort was not an issue requiring decision.[3] Palestine, the arena into which Jesus came, was occupied by Roman legions, into which the subject Jews, naturally enough, were not conscripted. At the most, many scholars have noted, since converts to "The Way" expected the early return of their Lord, their radical code was really an "interim ethic,"[4] unsuited to the demands of the long haul of history.

Be that as it may, the fourth century produced a radical mutation or paradigm shift in the definition of Christian faith and life.[5] That century opened with Christians subjected to the most severe of all the Imperial Roman persecutions. That same century ended, however, with the empire in the hands of Christians, with the persecut*ees* having become the persecut*ors*. Constantine (325–37) first legitimated and promoted Christianity in the Roman Empire, while Theodosius (379–95) made it the official Roman religion. Pagan cults were eventually suppressed, and by 412, only "Christians" were permitted in the Roman army. Some contemporaries, notably the bishop-historian Eusebius (died ca. 399) of Caesarea, were jubilant. Given the severe persecutions that some had suffered, this emotion is understandable.

But the larger import of the fourth-century change remains in dispute. Did the establishment of Christianity as the imperial religion constitute the "fall" of the church, as some historians claim, or its "triumph," as others have maintained?[6] Did the church fall *down*—or *up?* This much is clear: where initially the center of gravity of Christian action in the world lay in the regeneration of those thereby incorporated into the new community, it now shifted increasingly to investment in the external logic of a civilization. The fate of the religious and the political communities became inextricably linked.

Meanwhile, however, the empire, which was the agent of the Christian triumph, itself fell into decay. Following the fall of Rome (A.D. 476), monasteries, dioceses, parishes, and other Christian institutions filled some of the political, social, and economic void.[7] Clergy and churches became increasingly mired in temporal, even military, affairs. Political and military anarchy prevailed, and the doctrine of the just war evolved as a largely futile attempt to discipline and to restrain. The pacifism of the early Christians survived in the sometimes-violated immunity of the clergy from military service, and in occasional sectarian protest (the Waldensians, for example). But the pacifist option was generally absent from the official church or explicitly forbidden until the twentieth century.

The just-war doctrine, evolving over the centuries, dominated Christian thought for a full millennium, beginning with the fifth century. Renaissance, Reformation, and nationalism are the leading initial transformations said to lie between the medieval and the modern eras. Pacifist stirrings resurfaced briefly in the Renaissance and the Reformation (Anabaptists), but these stirrings were quickly squelched. The new national monarchies from the sixteenth century onward, presupposed, but also quickly manipulated, the just-war doctrine. The aspect of the doctrine legitimating military action could be invoked, while the strictures restraining it could be ignored. The resulting vulgarized version of the just-war doctrine that dominated the modern era was aptly summarized and transmitted in the familiar American dictum, "May she always be in the right; but our country, right or wrong" (Stephen Decatur, 1816).

The modern era, stretching from the sixteenth to the twentieth century, bears the onus of ever-wider wars, fought among nations comprising Christendom. Why, it may be asked, did not the concepts of human dignity, which inspired the modern democratic revolutions, result in a much earlier and greater outrage against war? Whatever the answer, not until the end of the Napoleonic Wars, the year of the Vienna Congress (1815) ending that epoch, did the first modern peace movement appear. Three peace societies were formed that year in the United States. The following year, 1816, saw the establishment of the British Society for the Promotion of Permanent and Universal Peace in London. Its purpose was to "print and circulate tracts and to diffuse information showing that *War* is inconsistent with the spirit of Christianity and the true interests of mankind. . . ."[8] In the United States, during the next few years, a number of local peace societies were formed, and, by 1828, the American Peace Society was established to oppose war on a broad basis. That society was to remain active until the latter part of the century.[9]

While the initial movements were rooted in religious soil, humanist inspiration operated as well. Typically, movement goals were issue-specific, permitting the cooperation of participants of varying persuasions, both religious and other. There are no grounds for Christians to claim exclusive credit (or blame!) for modern peace movements.

Since the early-nineteenth-century appearance of the first peace societies, a kind of cyclical rhythm can be discerned. Following each war, somewhat commensurate to its destructiveness, reaction sets in, and pacifist sentiment stirs anew. When the nation once more goes to war, most of this sentiment evaporates or goes underground. Over the past century, nonetheless, some cumulative momentum can be observed. Likewise, international interdependencies have grown rapidly, as have the lineaments of international organization. The International Court of Justice (The Hague), formed in 1899, the short-lived League of Nations, and the more durable, if still halting United Nations, represent advances toward global political order. Peace movements, though hardly the decisive dynamics underlying these developments, nonetheless contributed to the climate that made them possible, and, in turn, may be viewed as manifestations of a growing global awareness.

Though organized peace movements emerged early in the nineteenth century, not until after World War I did they become politically effective.[10] As the horror and the futility of that holocaust sank in, conviction mounted that war must—and can—be outlawed. Meanwhile, the force of nineteenth-century optimism was far from spent. From a marriage of dread and illusion was born a progeny of unrealistic schemes to rid the world of war. The churches for their part, now appalled at their complicity in the war (that story is told by Ray Abrams),[11] resolved, as Bainton observes, "to make every effort to see that there would never be another war to bless."[12]

Initially, these efforts appeared successful. In 1929 sixty-three nations signed an agreement, the Kellogg-Briand Pact, renouncing war as an instrument of national policy, and committing the signatories to the peaceful settlement of disputes. Pacifists were jubilant. The following year a major disarmament conference was held in London which declared a five-year holiday on capital shipbuilding and set tonnage limits for battleships. In 1934, the Oxford Union, the leading club of Oxford University, adopted the famous resolution, "This house will not fight for King and country." Revulsion at the horror and futility of the Great War (1914–18) combined with the legacy of nineteenth-century optimism to generate wholly unrealistic expectations.

Today we know that this "pacifist" victory was illusory. History, certainly in the then near future, was headed in a different direction. Nothing had happened structurally within nations, or in relations among them, to sustain the renunciations implicit in the Kellogg-Briand Pact. The key phrase in the agreement, "renunciation of war as an instrument of national policy," was itself vague. In any event, as Bainton observes, "all of the programs for the elimination of war rested on the assumption that man is good enough and wise enough to abolish war."[13] Not only were the results ephemeral, but critics charge that the "pacifism" of the 1920s and 1930s was self-defeating, that the disarming of the Western democracies produced the vacuum that Hitler filled. Had the Western democracies possessed the will and the might to resist him earlier, so the argument goes,

World War II could have been avoided. This interpretation became quasi doctrine in postwar American strategic policy. Disarmament brings war, not peace.[14]

Peace groups and movements, it must be reemphasized, were only a tributary to the wider stream of sentiment that sustained the disarmament initiatives of the post-World War I era. In the churches, the social gospel movement, which antedated World War I, had its own momentum, though it, too, had a strong pacifist penchant. During the 1930s, three thousand Protestant clergy, mostly from that movement, joined the Fellowship of Reconciliation. On the secular side, this was also a time of socialist internationalism. In a word, "pacifism" meant many things, as did "religion." Assessment of the era, and of the critics' verdicts on the era, requires a careful sifting of movements, actions, and policies. Undifferentiated indictments of the era serve no useful purpose. *Christian* pacifism entails dimensions of penitence, renunciation, and renewal that cannot be presupposed in the political arena, nor organized politically. On the other hand, to discredit disarmament efforts today because of the confusions and futilities of efforts in the 1920s and 1930s is both to misread the past and to mislead into the future.

THE EMERGENCE OF CHRISTIAN REALISM

Beneath the euphoria surrounding the supposed renunciation of war as an instrument of policy, not only was history in the short term moving in a different direction, but the social gospel, as it were, was generating its own "antibodies" against misguided pacifist optimism. Reinhold Niebuhr, an articulate young pastor who had been nurtured in the liberal and social gospel traditions, served in Detroit during the decade following World War I, the final years of the struggle of organized labor for recognition. In 1928, he left Detroit to join the faculty of Union Theological Seminary in New York.

Before moving to New York, Niebuhr had already become convinced that the liberal vision failed to confront the tragedy of power in society. His early work, *Moral Man and Immoral Society*, published in 1932, quickly became a classic. Where unselfishness is the highest ideal for the individual, Niebuhr argued, for the society the highest moral ideal is justice. He railed at "the moralists, both religious and secular," who ignore this distinction, and who fail to recognize that "when collective power, whether in the form of imperialism or class domination, exploits weakness, it can never be dislodged unless power is raised against it."[15]

Niebuhr, however, had early joined the Fellowship of Reconciliation, and in the 1920s, while in Detroit, he had become national chairman of the American branch of that organization. In his analysis of social class and conflict in American society during those years, he drew heavily on Marxist thought (on occasion he described himself as "Marxian"). On the other hand, his belief that international war was too destructive to contemplate kept him in the "pacifist" camp in international relations, long after his domestic reorientation was under way. In late 1933, however, the FOR polled its members to determine the extent to which pacifism was being defined in absolutist terms. In the wake of this survey, Niebuhr resigned as chairman, unable any longer to embrace an absolutist position. In an article entitled "Why I Leave the F.O.R.," Niebuhr made his decision public:

> Recognizing, as liberal Christianity does not, that the world of politics is full of demonic forces we have chosen on the whole to support the devil of vengeance against the devil of hypocrisy. In the day in which we live a dying social system commits the hypocrisy of hiding its injustices behind the forms of justice and the victims of injustice express their politics in terms of resentment against this injustice. As Marxians we support this resentment against the hypocrisy. As Christians we know there is a devil in the spirit of vengeance as well as in the spirit of hypocrisy. For that reason we respect those who try to have no traffic with devils at all.[16]

Despite the enormous change in thought that had taken place, however, Niebuhr in 1934 had not yet fully reversed his position. Elsewhere in his statement, he asserted that "I am forced to associate myself with the 20 percent of the fellowship who are pacifists only in the sense that they will refuse to participate in an international armed conflict. Perhaps it would clear the issue if we admitted that we were not pacifists at all. We probably all recognize the terrible possibilities of violence. *We regard an international armed conflict as so suicidal that we are certain that we will not participate in it*" (italics added).[17]

By 1941, however, some months before Pearl Harbor, he joined others in launching *Christianity and Crisis,* the journal which became the mouthpiece for the reorientation in thought that came to be known as "Christian realism." In his opening editorial, Niebuhr identified two schools of thought, one believing that "war could be eliminated if only Christians and other men of good will refused resolutely enough to have anything to do with conflict." Another school, he wrote, holds that "there are historic situations in which refusal to defend the inheritance of a civilization, however imperfect, against tyranny and aggression may result in consequences even worse than war. This journal intends to express and, if possible, to clarify this second viewpoint." "Christian realism," with Niebuhr as its most effective spokesman, was to gird the American churches, and American opinion far beyond, for the "tragic" ordeal of World War II. Hans Morgenthau, the dean of American political scientists for some years, wrote later of Niebuhr, "I have always considered Reinhold Niebuhr the greatest living philosopher of America, perhaps the only creative political philosopher since Calhoun."[18]

Christian realism succeeded in stamping an entire era. Apart from a vigorous but numerically small community of conscientious objectors, pacifist voices during World War II were largely muffled. Several years were to elapse after the war before they once more were to find a common voice, and it is to that pacifist revival that we now turn.

THE OXFORD CONFERENCE AND THE ECUMENICAL MOVEMENT

The pacifisms of the 1920s and 1930s, and the Christian realist response of the 1940s were not the only important developments during this era. Among the non-Roman Christian communions, several important ecumenical conversations were in progress. While these did not stem the tide toward what turned out to be a second "world war," the conversation and the movement it presaged survived. An ecumenical conference on "Church, Community and the State," held at Oxford in 1937, signaled the coming shift of the attitude of the churches toward war. Summoning the "church to be the church," the conference identified three main positions prevalent in the churches with regard to war. "Some believe," the report read, that "especially in its modern form, war is always sin. . . . Some would participate only in just wars . . . , [and finally] some, while also stressing the Christian obligation to work for peace and mutual understanding among nations, hold, nonetheless, that no such effort can end war in this world." None of these three positions, the statement observes, can claim to "represent the only Christian attitude." Rather, the perplexity arising from these disagreements "is in itself a sign of the sin in which its [the church's] members are implicated." In view of this fact, the church cannot "rest in permanent acquiescence in the continuance of these differences but should do all that is possible to promote the study of the problem by people of different views meeting together to learn from one another as they seek to understand the purpose of God as revealed in Jesus Christ."[19] The lack of a common Christian practice and witness with regard to war and peace was attributed simply to human failure, rather than, as so often in the past, either to divine inscrutability or to the human condition.

Oxford paved the way for the positions espoused by the World Council of Churches in the founding Assembly of Amsterdam in 1948. Though Amsterdam may have meant a partial retreat from advances notable at Oxford—the impact of both the war and Christian realism could be felt— the dawn of the nuclear age between Oxford and Amsterdam released new impulses. Moreover, it was evident that Christian disunity was not only an ecclesiastical or a sacramental problem. More scandalous than sacramental disunity were the recurrent wars of "Christendom."

Building on Oxford, the appropriate section of the Amsterdam WCC Assembly report began, "War is contrary to the will of God." Once more three positions were identified: the just war, the pacifist, and then, registering the dawning of the nuclear age (1945) in the interim since Oxford (1937), a new position held by those who believe that "modern warfare, with its mass destruction, can never be an act of justice."[20] "Nuclear pacifism" was aborning. Though the dominant influence of the just-war doctrine was still evident throughout the report, for the first time in the modern context, pacifism was restored explicitly by the major communions as a legitimate Christian option.

Analogous developments were to follow on the Roman Catholic side less than two decades later. First came the encyclical, *Pacem in Terris* (1963), and then decisions of the Vatican II Council. "Any act of war aimed indiscriminately at the destruction of entire cities or extensive areas along with their population," declared one of the council documents, "is a crime against God and man himself. It merits unequivocal and unhesitating condemnation." Though with greater qualification than the Oxford and the WCC statements, Vatican II also offered support for the conscientious objector to military service. In any case, pacifism now became an option within the Roman Catholic tradition as well.[21] The pacifist paradigm of the early church has been restored as a valid option in the life, the dialogue, and the witness of the church.

CONVERTING THE CHURCH TO PACIFISM?

Meanwhile, pacifists once more bestirred themselves. In 1950, nearly four hundred church persons, mostly pacifist, gathered in Detroit in a four-day national conference on "the church and war." Planned by an ad hoc committee composed of Fellowship of Reconciliation, peace church, and denominational peace group representatives, the conference was more than a year in the making. According to *The Christian Century* (May 24, 1950), it was the first large postwar gathering of Christian pacifists in the United States.

Two important developments facilitated and perhaps triggered the Detroit initiative. The first was the rapid crystallization, in the late 1940s, of the cold war. In Eastern Europe, the Soviet Union was consolidating the band of buffer states to its west, the embodiment of the strategic doctrine that it derived from its experience in World War II. In the West, the Marshall Plan had been launched in 1948, and the following year, the North Atlantic Treaty Organization (NATO) was formed. More seriously, though the notorious Pacific thermonuclear tests of the 1950s were still more than a year away, and antecedent developments were secret, the threat of coming events was already casting a shadow. According to some pacifists, it was time to signal the dangers ahead.

The other antecedent development was a hopeful one. As noted above, the World Council of Churches had just been formed, and pacifist church people were keenly aware of both the Oxford and the Amsterdam declarations. If the atomic threat made action urgent, the ecumenical movement appeared to make it possible. Nonetheless, the purposes of the May 1950 event in Detroit were somewhat vague. After planning had been under way for more than six months, John Oliver Nelson, chairman of the planning committee, in a meeting of that group in 1949, observed that "the Conference was originally thought of as a means of studying more fully the third position of the Amsterdam Conference of the World Council of Churches"[22] ("others, again, refuse military service of all kinds . . ."). Now legitimated as a valid Christian option, pacifism, it was implied, had to rework its agenda.

But the summons for pacifists to reformulate their self-understanding was not an end in itself. Earlier planning-committee agenda minutes observed that the proposed conference "would be one of church people, with church orientation, speaking to the church but would not be an officially delegated church conference . . . [that it would] attempt to present the dilemma which faces the church when, in the atomic age, it is divided on the crucial question of war." As the Oxford Conference had pointed out, the variety of opinions in the church on this issue is itself an evidence of sin. What, then, can the churches do about it?[23]

While the Detroit event did not fully meet the organizers' expectations,[24] it generated considerable encouragement and enthusiasm among the participants. The work of the conference fell into three broad areas, theological, social and political, and practical. Perhaps the most important product of the gathering was a theological tract of some forty pages published under the title "A Christian Approach to Nuclear War." Originally signed by a committee of thirty leaders in the Detroit gathering, it was cosigned later by hundreds of ministers. This tract went through a number of printings, and eventually forty thousand copies were distributed. This document, sober and evangelical in tone, was further evidence that pacifists had learned, both from the tragedies of the era and from their chatisement by "Christian realism."[25]

A continuing organization, "The Church Peace Mission" (CPM), was formed to reach the churches throughout the country with the Detroit message, and in fact to ask them "to break with war." A. J. Muste, then the executive officer of the FOR, stated in the initial proposal that "the object of the Mission . . . is to make pacifism articulate in the church." Minutes of the first executive committee meeting were more direct; the aim of the CPM was said to be to "convert the church." In the same breath, however, it was also noted, likely in anticipation of criticism, that the Mission was "opposed to totalitarianism and violence." During 1950 and 1951, a dozen regional consultations were held across the U.S., and several important studies were commissioned.

The CPM confronted basic problems from the outset. Its stated goals would have required a far deeper pooling of energies, resources, and structures among the supporting constituencies than was ever in the offing. In a small way, the problem paralleled that of the World Council of Churches: initially, the grandeur of the vision appears to carry everything before it, until there is time for rebound from constituent member interests. The CPM reached this critical point by the end of the second year, when the executive director of the Mission, J. Martin England, reported a fundamental organizational change. While the sponsoring organizations were to continue the appointment of representatives to the executive committee, "individual projects hereafter would be carried out by the organizations themselves, rather than by a paid Church Peace Mission staff."[26] That decision indicated clearly that the original goal was beyond reach.

A second national rally, this one convened directly by the CPM, was held in Detroit in December 1953. Considerable attention was devoted to the then-forthcoming Second Assembly of the World Council of Churches (Evanston, summer, 1954). Steps were set in motion to contact delegates and to seek stronger action toward peace by the Assembly. Such CPM efforts to engage the WCC peaked with that Assembly, though some contacts continued throughout the decade. Meanwhile, the "Puidoux Conference," a Europe-based dialogue between pacifist and nonpacifist scholars, to which the CPM had ties, had more direct access to the WCC staff.[27] The CPM coordinated its efforts with, and after the Evanston meeting deferred to, that group.

The CPM held two more national gatherings during the 1950s, one a youth conference, but otherwise continued a more limited program—colloquies, studies, pamphlets, sermon contests, and the like—until the end of the decade. One important venture during this time, undertaken jointly with Christian Action (a Niebuhrian circle) ended as CA disbanded, and the papers from both sides, many of them already completed, became archival material.[28]

A. J. MUSTE—A PACIFIST'S PACIFIST

Even a fragmentary account of the CPM such as this is incomplete without a profile of A. J. Muste (1885-1967) who, more than anyone else, was the moving spirit behind both the 1950 Detroit Conference on the Church and War and the Church Peace Mission to which it gave birth. Muste was at once an ordained Presbyterian minister (on inactive status) and a Quaker. Discovery of the writings of the Christian mystics and the Anabaptists led the young minister to become a pacifist during World War I. A labor organizer by the early 1920s, already in conversation with Reinhold Neibuhr, Muste became a Marxist. But since he understood Christianity as intrinsically nonviolent, and Marxism as tied intrinsically to revolutionary violence, he felt constrained to abandon the former. Yet, not for long. By 1936, having found the strain of violence in Marxism repugnant, Muste abandoned Marx to return definitively to his earlier faith.[29] Christian nonviolence clearly had deeper roots in Muste's soul.

Throughout his long life, Muste initiated and participated in many causes and organizations, most of them outside the "organized church." Mutually critical and respectful of each other's polar positions, the two contemporaries, Muste and Niebuhr, played somewhat analogous roles within their respective constituencies. Muste was a remarkable blend of a flaming Hebrew prophet and the meek man from Nazareth. Alienated from the organized church in the sense that he could not wait for it to shake off its shackles, he acted with others outside the church who responded to the prophetic mandate. Yet, he remained at heart a Christian and even a churchman. Like an importunate lover, he responded when something seemed afoot in the churches. Thus, he followed with hopeful interest the theological conversations in the National and World Councils of Churches, as these pertained to international peace and justice. During the CPM years, he corresponded widely with theologians and clergy.[30] Perhaps more than any venture, proposing *a mission to the churches* expressed both the closeness and the distance that he felt.

THE END OF A MISSION

By the late 1950s, the goals of the CPM had been "displaced": the original Church and War Conference of 1950 sought a reconstitution of pacifist thought whereas the CPM, which it fathered, sought to convert the church. That goal being quite beyond reach, there remained among the original objectives, the possibility of dialogue with representatives of the other two positions outlined at Amsterdam: those holding that since military action is the ultimate sanction of the rule of law, it is the duty of citizens "to defend the law by force if necessary," and those adhering to what was coming to be known as nuclear pacifism.

The fourth and last of the CPM national conferences held in 1959 sought particularly to engage the latter group, the "nuclear pacifists," in dialogue. This choice may have been tactical in part for if, as the Amsterdam report noted, nuclear pacifists held that "modern warfare, with its mass destruction, can never be an act of justice," persons who have moved to that position (presumably from the just-war camp), might be persuaded thereupon to take the final step to full pacifism! But there were deeper reasons for the choice. The concern was genuine: Who, indeed, could pretend to have "the" answer to the nuclear threat then engulfing humankind? Who could claim to embody precisely "the" form of Christian obedience in such a world? But the 1959 conference, like its predecessors, led to no major breakthrough.

The CPM now turned to its final option—dialogue with the dominant nonpacifist tradition within the churches. This decision resulted in a modest five-year program of smaller colloquies and publications, mostly in or related to theological seminaries. Initially ecumenically Protestant, it soon drew in Roman Catholics as well, along with occasional Jewish contacts. By the mid-1960s, however, Vatican II had met, the civil-rights movement was at flood tide, and controversies over the growing war in Vietnam were heating up. Action now seemed more important than recondite dialogue. In August 1967, the CPM was terminated.[31]

THE WAR-NATION-CHURCH STUDY GROUP

In the early 1960s, the CPM had assembled a small advisory committee of ethicists which over the next few years developed a life of its own. With the blessing of the retiring CPM, this group decided to enlarge its membership and to stay together. It adopted as its own the name of the CPM monthly bulletin, becoming, thus, the War-Nation-Church Study Group (WANACH). Its purpose became the continuation and deepening of a church-centered pacifist-nonpacifist dialogue among Christian ethicists.

The WANACH group, now numbering some twenty members, continued into the 1980s, meeting annually for two days in Washington, D.C. Each meeting, with a prepared agenda, chooses the problems to be treated the following year. Members report on scholarship work and other experiences during the previous year. On occasion, a guest expert may be invited to treat a particular topic. Issues of war and peace are explored in terms of the pacifist-nonpacifist tension in the Christian tradition. Neither exponent seeks to convert the other. A line of accountability to the churches is maintained as support comes from denominational agencies—Brethren, Lutheran, Mennonite, Presbyterian, and Roman Catholic.

Consider an excerpt from a WANACH session in 1970. Charles West had probed alternatives between reform and revolution:

In the ensuing discussion, questions were raised concerning the legitimacy of the state to rule, which did not seem clear in West's presentation. West restated his problem as the search for a view of order which permits positive expression for the one dehumanized by it, but an expression which will not forget the need to keep the enemy within the relationship. Paul's admonition to pray for authorities assumes that God is creating some kind of order through the covenant. But, even if the state lacks legitimacy, the people can be conditioned to question nothing: what is, must be (Monika Hellwig). But the problem, West replied, is that people live with a concept of eternal order, but with no concept of covenant. In such a society, the preaching of the gospel tends to break things up. A regime may have the power to conquer a nation without possessing the power to organize a society. If I were a Christian in the Soviet Union, I'd live by the hope that the society would open sufficiently for covenant-based communities to emerge within it (West). But what of Latin America and Africa (Thomas Heath)? Would you ever take a gun (David Little)? I might (West). But how would you reconcile that with the view that the enemy must be kept within the covenant (Hellwig)? The deterrent effect of such an act, coupled with the readiness of the opponent to yield ground, may be the beginning of covenant enactment (West). But am I to stop killing with killing? What is the covenant with the ones I am killing (Hellwig)? No answer—only the forgiveness of God? West turns the question back to Hellwig, who likewise is uncertain, but feels pushed more and more to give a pacifist answer. Hehir: So you have a value scale which permits the violation of every value except life? Hellwig: I can find no basis upon which to make such a judgment instead of God. West, accepting the dictum, Who am I to play God?, therefore finds himself extremely reluctant, except for the most extreme necessity, to act against the life of another, and then only in penance and appeal to grace. But the real meaning of penance was always that I might have done otherwise and didn't (John Howard Yoder). Whereupon Hellwig: Is the concept of tangible guilt essential to *metanoia*? *Metanoia* means, said West, given the situation I have created, what do I do now? The discussion ended with an exchange concerning filial and covenantal categories, with the offertory seen as contract and the communion as gift.[32]

OUTCOMES OF HONEST EXCHANGE

What happens when, as in this exchange, pacifist and nonpacifist Christians take one another seriously? What are the issues that crystallize between them? What outcomes can be awaited? At most, WANACH has probably done advance reconnoitering, looking to a time when such dialogue will assume central importance in the churches.

The WANACH dialogue illustrates once more the fact that the pacifist-nonpacifist disagreement reaches to the heart of the major tenets of the faith itself, to the central affirmations concerning salvation and redemption. Each seems to purchase the clarity and validity of its position at the expense of other aspects of the biblical message. To put the difference aside as secondary, as one of the adiaphora, left to the personal taste of the believer, is simply to trivialize and confuse the issue. Early agreement between the two views theologically is unlikely, perhaps even undesirable, yet the issue is both fundamental and urgent.

More importantly, however, the possibility of fruitful and sustained encounter between the two traditions is not only a tribute to a more tolerant age, though it is that, but is above all a function of historic change. Though tenacious vestiges persist, the churches generally have been "disestablished." Christendom as civilization has passed. As pacifism was surpassed many centuries ago, so too the just-war tradition is being surpassed along with the Christendom that nurtured it. Both pacifism and nonpacifism are now disestablished options, competing with other value systems in a pluralistic universe. Moreover, despite the deep differences just noted, the nuclear threat, and other challenges of the modern world, crystallized to an unprecedented degree the substance of faith which they share in common, a faith which must assert itself in the face of the obscenities of an arms race out of control.

The history that is rapidly bringing the two traditions into dialogue also in part constitutes the agenda itself. In some respects, the era of global experience that we have now entered resembles more nearly the early centuries than it does the Christendom era of recent centuries.

THE CHURCH RE-SECTARIANIZED?

Sociologically speaking, the churches, at least in the Western world, have been returned to a "sectarian" position within society;[33] that is, they represent one of many value options available to a population, rather than the dominant mode. Less and less can they rely on monopoly or even a favored position in the symbolic universe. Accordingly, *witness* rather than *control* becomes once more, as in the New Testament, the basic mode of the Christian presence in the world.

This "re-sectarianizing" of the church in the world is fraught with peril, a peril to which the heirs of the just-war tradition are particularly sensitive. Basically, the just-war doctrine, as restated in the language of Christian realism, views the enforcement of justice and order as the specification of the works of love in the public sphere.[34] The early Christian communities, though constrained by a compassionate missionary zeal, concentrated their ethical energies on the interior life of the bands of disciples. A minority position of this sort, however, readily translates into a spirit of withdrawal or a ghetto mentality among Christians.

In a second way, history constitutes the agenda for the pacifist-nonpacifist encounter: namely, by the threat of nuclear mass destruction. It is ironical, when the just-war doctrine is suddenly taken seriously (nuclear weapons are renounced because they exceed all bounds which might make war conditionally "just"), that many Christians brought up in that tradition are ready to abandon it. Perhaps their real frustration is the blame they place, rightly or wrongly, on the doctrine for legitimating a system that gave rise to the nuclear dilemma in the first place.

Be that as it may, the moment nuclear weapons are renounced on the basis of the just-war doctrine itself, the believer finds him- or herself in the same eschatological position in which the traditional pacifist has always stood. "We are prepared to risk defeat in history because of faith in, and commitment to, a higher kingdom." While this posture can lead to resignation or escapism, that is not its intrinsic meaning. Few nuclear pacifists or just-war objectors sense or understand the new eschatology into which they have been catapulted. Here is one rather concrete and potentially fruitful area for a common and mutually instructive search by pacifists and nonpacifists.

Finally, if all this means in fact a renewed engagement with the basic

41

categories of the faith, it results in a gain for all concerned. Obstacles, to be sure, are enormous, though this is not the place for their enumeration. The pluralization of theology and faith is clearly a corollary of the pluralization of the culture.[35] Less and less can we presuppose cultural reinforcement of faith categories by the culture. The Bible is increasingly remote, and even many Christians find it to be hardly an accessible and authoritative source of guidance.

To dwell only on these features of our age, however, is truly to miss "the signs of the times." Undoubtedly, for many the encounter between Christianity and the forces of the modern world has been costly. Whether one thinks of historical forces such as the industrial and the political revolutions, or of intellectual currents represented by names such as Darwin, Marx, and Freud, the faith has "taken a beating." But this has been a means of liberation and purification of the faith. Laying bare the historical relativities of the biblical saga has also exposed the profound significance of the Judeo-Christian prophetic tradition, of which Abraham serves as a prototype.[36]

We have access today to a broader and more mature grasp of that faith and its significance than has ever before been possible. It is true, of course, as in scientific knowledge generally, that (to reverse a common saying) the whole is less than the sum of the parts. That is, we have knowledge far more detailed and specialized than what becomes available in configurations that are usable in the common life. Coining the idioms of action to bridge these gaps is a critical task for our generation.[37] Any new movement for peace in the churches is hostage to such bridgebuilding as well as to the pacifist-nonpacifist dialogue. Until there is a broad, a fundamental, or a principled commitment to peace, government officials can only manipulate, and the arms race will continue.

NOTES

1. Roland H. Bainton, *Christian Attitudes Toward War and Peace* (Nashville and New York: Abingdon Press, 1960).

2. 1 Peter 2:21, 23.

3. Oscar Cullman, *Jesus and the Revolutionaries* (New York: Harper & Row, 1970).

4. The classic treatment of this theme was Albert Schweitzer's *The Quest of the Historical Jesus* (New York: Macmillan Co., 1961). Cf. also Ray C. Petry, *Christian Eschatology and Social Thought* (Nashville and New York: Abingdon Press, 1965).

5. The concepts of "paradigm" and of "paradigm shift," to refer to domi-

nant models of understanding and/or methodology, were developed by Thomas Kuhn, *The Structure of Scientific Revolutions* (Chicago and London: University of Chicago Press, 1970). The conceptions have proved fertile as seen in the discussions they have triggered meanwhile in many disciplines. Here we refer to the typical and, hence, ruling configurations of general definitions of the Christian faith.

6. G. J. Heering, *The Fall of Christianity* (New York: Fellowship Publications, 1943); Shirley Jackson Case, *The Social Triumph of Early Christianity* (New York: Harper & Brothers, 1933).

7. The early Middle Ages show striking, and likely instructive, parallels to base-communities phenomena in Latin America and elsewhere, and to the liberation theology linked to them. In a time of political anarchy, monasteries and parishes in the early medieval era offered the only centers of stability and security. But we need to ask: to what extent did the eventual militarization of Christianity spring from the quite understandable actions of "self-defense"? Can a careful study of that era in Europe provide any guidance to liberation theologians today? Someone needs to find out!

8. Norman Angell, "Peace Movements," *Encyclopedia of the Social Sciences* (New York: Macmillan Co., 1933), 12:41–47. For a fuller treatment, see Peter Brock, *Pacifism in the United States: From the Colonial Era to the First World War* (Princeton: Princeton University Press, 1968).

9. Peter Brock, "The American Peace Society: The First Decade," in *Pacifism in the United States*, chap. 11.

10. Peter Brock, *Twentieth Century Pacifism: New Perspectives in Political Science* (New York: D. Van Nostrand, 1970), 2.

11. Ray Abrams, *Preachers Present Arms* (New York: Round Table Press, 1933).

12. Bainton, *Christian Attitudes Toward War and Peace*, 214.

13. Ibid.

14. For example, see Telford Taylor, *Munich: The Price of Peace* (Garden City, N.Y.: Doubleday & Co., 1979).

15. Reinhold Niebuhr, *Moral Man and Immoral Society* (New York: Charles Scribner's Sons, 1960 [1932]).

16. Reinhold Niebuhr, "Why I Leave the F.O.R.," *The Christian Century* (January 3, 1934).

17. Ibid.

18. Ronald Stone, *Reinhold Niebuhr: Prophet to Politicians* (Nashville and New York: Abingdon Press, 1972), 9.

19. J. H. Oldham, ed., *The Oxford Conference: Official Report* (Chicago: Willett & Clark, 1938), 162–63.

20. In the three positions sketched by the First Assembly of the World Council of Churches (Amsterdam, 1948) the just-war position (Oxford's second) became in effect what was later known as "pacifism." It was listed first and read, "There are those who hold that even though entering a war may be a Christian's duty in particular circumstances, modern warfare, with its mass destruction, can never

be an act of justice." W. A. Visser 't Hooft, ed., *The First Assembly of the World Council of Churches* (London: SCM Press, 1949).

21. This quotation comes from the document entitled the "Pastoral Constitution on the Church in the Modern World," in *The Documents of Vatican II,* ed. Walter M. Abbott, S.J. (New York: Guild Press, 1966), 294. On conscientious objection, see p. 292. For a contemporary discussion, see the essay by J. Bryan Hehir below.

22. Minutes and other records of the conference and planning have been deposited in the Swarthmore College Peace Collection classified under "Church Peace Mission."

23. CPM file, Swarthmore College Peace Collection. In the same collection, see also the A. J. Muste files (microfilm AJM 89.8, 9, 10). Quoted by permission.

24. Compare the announcement in an unsigned editorial in *The Christian Century* 67 (May 10, 1950) with the *Century* editor's report on the meeting. Harold Fey, "Pacifist Christians Call on the Church to Break with War," *The Christian Century* 67 (May 24, 1950): 652–53.

25. *The Christian Conscience and War* (New York: The Church Peace Mission, [1951]).

26. Letter from J. Martin England to W. W. Wittcamper, dated September 2, 1952. CPM file, Swarthmore College Peace Collection, cited by permission.

27. Donald F. Durnbaugh, ed., *On Earth Peace: Discussions on War/Peace Issues Between Friends, Mennonites, Brethren and European Churches 1935–1975* (Elgin, Ill.: The Brethren Press, 1978).

28. The file of papers is in the possession of the chairman of the joint committee representing Christian Action, Edward Le Roy Long, Jr., currently of Drew Theological Seminary. The files of Christian Action are in the custody of Robert Handy, Union Theological Seminary, New York.

29. Jo Ann O. Robinson, *Abraham Went Out: A Biography of A. J. Muste* (Philadelphia: Temple University Press, 1982); Nat Hentoff, ed., *The Essays of A. J. Muste* (New York: Simon & Schuster, 1970); also by Hentoff, *Peace Agitator: The Story of A. J. Muste,* rev. ed. (New York: A. J. Muste Memorial Institute, 1982). The Robinson volume reached me only after this chapter was written.

30. Before and after the major CPM events, and on occasions such as the Second Assembly of the WCC in Evanston (1954), Muste wrote many letters to prominent churchmen and theologians, and received numerous, sometimes detailed replies (tapes 89.8, 9, 10 in the Swarthmore College Peace Collection, cited by permission). These are important because they demonstrate his continued sense of identity with the church in its profound sense, despite his institutional distance, and his active collaboration with many extra-ecclesial groups.

31. A set of August 1967 minutes of the F.O.R. (Muste file, Swarthmore College Peace Collection) simply notes that as of that date CPM activities have been discontinued.

32. A complete set of notes on the advisory committee and the subsequent WANACH sessions is in possession of the writer. The files of the Church Peace Mission for the period 1961–67, once stored in the Methodist Building in Washington, D.C., have apparently been lost.

33. Cf. Ernst Troeltsch's classic, *The Social Teaching of the Christian Churches* (New York: Harper Torchbooks, 1960 [1931]). George Lindbeck offers a contemporary reflection on the changing position of the churches in the modern world in "The Sectarian Future of the Church," in *The God Experience: Essays in Hope*, ed. Joseph P. Whalen, S.J. (Paramus, N.J.: Newman Press, 1971), 226–43.

34. Paul Ramsey, initially something of a "voice in the wilderness," espoused this point at a time when little formal attention was given to the precise maxims of the just-war doctrine. See especially his *War and the Christian Conscience: How Shall Modern War Be Conducted Justly?* (Durham, N.C.: Duke University Press, 1961).

35. David Tracy's *Blessed Rage for Order* (New York: Seabury Press, 1975) is an important theological response to the pluralist challenge. (See also Tracy's *Analogical Imagination* [New York: Crossroad, 1981]).

36. For a stimulating treatment of the significance of Abraham by a contemporary Jewish writer, see Silvano Arieti, *Abraham and the Contemporary Mind* (New York: Basic Books, 1981).

37. Some of these problems quickly surfaced when in the CPM study program in the early 1960s an attempt was made to establish a crossover between the renewal in biblical thought sometimes known as "biblical realism" (best known in the U.S.A. in the scholarship descended from the work of W. F. Albright at Johns Hopkins University). On the CPM venture see *Biblical Realism Confronts the Nation*, ed. Paul Peachey (Nyack, N.Y.: Fellowship Publications, 1963).

3

CHURCH-TYPE REINVIGORATED: THE BISHOPS' LETTER

J. BRYAN HEHIR

The Roman Catholic Church is the classical model of what Ernst Troeltsch defined as a "church-type." In its theology, polity, and practice the Catholic Church fulfilled the church-type model for centuries before Troeltsch analyzed the phenomenon. The basic elements of Troeltsch's analysis have been accepted by scholars inside and outside the Catholic community.[1] But the extent of the theological and institutional changes that have marked Catholicism since the Second Vatican Council makes it useful to ask if it still fits Troeltsch's model of the church-type polity. I will analyze the question of contemporary Catholicism as a church-type by focusing on the pastoral letter of the U.S. Bishops, *The Challenge of Peace: God's Promise and Our Response*, published in 1983.[2]

For Troeltsch the question of war provided one of the clearest examples of how a church related its moral vision to its sense of ecclesial identity. The pastoral letter tests Catholic moral teaching, the church's understanding of its role in society, and the meaning of discipleship in light of the revolutionary challenge posed by nuclear weapons. The pastoral letter is a case study that illustrates the present state of Catholic teaching in light of the developments in the church caused by Vatican II and the changes in the world wrought by the nuclear age. I will also examine how Vatican II prepared the way for *The Challenge of Peace*, where the pastoral moved beyond Vatican II, and, finally, what themes will shape the future direction of the church's public role in the United States.

Fr. J. Bryan Hehir, long-time (1973-83) director of the Office of International Justice and Peace, U.S. Catholic Conference, Washington, D.C., is now secretary of Social Development and World Peace, USCC, and senior research scholar, Kennedy Institute of Ethics, Georgetown University.

FROM THE PASTORAL CONSTITUTION
TO THE PASTORAL LETTER

At the outset of the pastoral letter the U.S. Bishops acknowledge their direct dependence upon the teaching of the Second Vatican Council:

> The Catholic tradition on war and peace is a long and complex one reaching from the Sermon on the Mount to the statements of Pope John Paul II. . . . As we locate ourselves in this tradition, seeking to draw from it and to develop it, the document which provides profound inspiration and guidance for us is *The Pastoral Constitution on the Church in the Modern World* of Vatican II, for it is based on doctrinal principles and addresses the relationship of the Church to the world with respect to the most urgent issues of our day.[3]

The pastoral letter stands in the direct line of Vatican II, ecclesiologically, morally, and politically. Moreover, the *Pastoral Constitution* is the most authoritative and extensive contemporary statement of Catholic teaching on the relationship of the church to the world. For both of these reasons, the ecclesiology of the Pastoral Constitution is a precondition for understanding the perspective of the pastoral letter.

The full ecclesiology of Vatican II can be assessed only in light of its sixteen documents, but the church-world problematic is found in two texts: the *Pastoral Constitution* and the *Declaration on Religious Liberty*.[4] Troeltsch defined "the new social question" of the twentieth century in terms of this church-state and church-society distinction. The Vatican Council used precisely this distinction to articulate its theology of the church in the world. The church-state relationship is the subject of the *Declaration*; the church-society question is the subject of the *Pastoral Constitution*. The two documents must be read in tandem but they also must be analyzed in light of the distinct contribution each makes to the contemporary Catholic understanding of the church's role in the world.

The basic contribution of the *Declaration* was to clarify the Catholic position on the role of the state in society, particularly as it touched upon religious issues. Catholic teaching since the Reformation had been shaped by the theory of "the Catholic state." The theory asserted the obligation of the state to recognize a special status in civil law for the Catholic religion in countries with a predominantly Catholic population. Although parallel examples could be found in Protestant nations, the theology of a religion of the state had assumed a more visible posture in Catholic theology.[5] The First Vatican Council (1879) had formulated the church-state question in terms of the "Thesis/Hypothesis" distinction. The "thesis" or normative position called for a special status for Catholicism and restrictions on the public expressions of other faith communities in a "Catholic state." The "hypothesis" was the relationship that could be "tolerated" in those countries where, because of demography, culture, or history, the attempt to institute "a Catholic state" would be counterproductive.

John Courtney Murray, the principal author of the *Declaration*, argued that the fundamental purpose of the teaching of Vatican II was to recast—indeed to replace—the formula of Vatican I as the controlling concept of church-state relations. The conditions of the twentieth century, Murray contended, were sufficiently different from the sixteenth or nineteenth centuries that a new statement of Catholic teaching, made at the level of theological principle, was needed to assert the Catholic understanding of religious liberty and church-state relations.

The content of the *Declaration* can be summarized in three propositions. First, it affirmed the right of religious liberty as a basic human right to be recognized for each person by the church and the state. Second, it affirmed Catholic recognition of the secularity of the state. This assertion (which would have surprised Troeltsch) involved two subordinate propositions. On the one hand, the secularity of the state involves a recognition of the independence of the state from religious tutelage, a recognition by the church of the legitimate and positive role the state plays in society. On the other hand, the scope of the state's role is limited by a series of factors: the human rights of the person that precede the state; the constitutional law of a society that should both empower the state to act and set limits to its action; and the rights and role of other independent institutions—voluntary associations and religious communities—that do not owe their origin or existence to the power of the state.

Third, the *Declaration* defines the relationship of the church to the state in terms of freedom, not favoritism for the church. In a striking contrast to the formulation of Vatican I, the *Declaration* asserts that the fundamental requirement of church-state relations is "the freedom of the church" to fulfill its ministry. With these three principles established (the right of religious liberty, the secularity of the state, and the freedom of the church) the Second Vatican Council then turned to the broader question of the church's role in society.

Throughout the conciliar debate on religious liberty Murray stressed the critical but limited purpose of the *Declaration*. It resolved the nineteenth-century dispute about church and state in terms of the juridical and institutional questions proper to that conflict. The twentieth-century question is the relationship of the church to the rest of society, that is, everything lying beyond the scope of the state. The logic of this relationship is not juridical or institutional, but pastoral and "political" in the sense of a concern for ordering the life of society. The conclusions of the *Declaration* were contemporary and new but the concepts had the flavor of the ancient church-state argument.

Both the style and the substance of the *Pastoral Constitution*, on the other hand, broke new ground in Catholic theology. The church-society relationship is analyzed in terms that are classical in character but contemporary in tone. The Augustinian "two-cities" theme is the foundation of the chapter on the "Church in the World" but the description of the church's collaboration with other institutions in society is more positive than Augustinian theology. The conciliar document reflects traditional Catholic social philosophy that both society and state are the products of the social nature of the person and play a positive role in the history of salvation.

The distinctive contribution of the *Pastoral Constitution* is the way it takes the "incarnational" themes that run through christology, ecclesiology, and sacramentology in Catholic thought and weaves them into a strong endorsement of the church's role in the world. The first four chapters of the *Pastoral Constitution* are a reflection on the meaning of the incarnation for the history of the world and for the human person, the center of human history. The mystery of the incarnation transforms our understanding of human dignity (#22); it deepens our sense of human community and solidarity (#32); it gives new dignity to human work and culture (#39); and it provides the basis for the church's salvific ministry in history (#45).

None of these "incarnational" themes was new, but the presentation of them in a systematic fashion provided a more developed ecclesiology for the social ministry of the church than any previous magisterial document. The *Pastoral Constitution* did not significantly add to the specific analysis of social issues found in the papal social encyclicals from Leo XIII (died 1903) to John XXIII (died 1963), but it established a much stronger rationale and impetus for all that the social encyclicals had said.

The *Pastoral Constitution* has had a substantial impact since the Vatican Council. Its pastoral-political substance has been joined to a style of ecclesial presence in the world most dramatically represented by the public ministry of John Paul II but also reflected at the local level of the church's life. The pastoral activity endorsed by the conciliar text quickly takes on a "political" character for the church. The linkage of the pastoral and political is captured in a key passage of the document:

> In pursuing its own salvific purpose not only does the church communicate divine life to men but in a certain sense it casts the reflected light of that

divine life over all the earth, notably in the way it heals and elevates the dignity of the human person, in the way it consolidates society and endows the daily activity of men with a deeper sense and meaning.[6]

This sentence provides the basis for the church's "indirect" influence on the political process. To address questions of human dignity, human rights, and the meaning of secular activity involves the church in specific questions of the political, economic, and international order. The church is political in its ultimate influence but not explicitly political in its mode of activity. The *Pastoral Constitution* has pushed the church to be a "public church," something different from a "political church."

Would Troeltsch recognize in the contemporary public church his church-type model? Both the *Declaration* and the *Pastoral Constitution* reaffirm the main lines of a church-type theology and polity. The church's sense of responsibility for the whole of society is, if anything, intensified by the theology of Vatican II. The structure of church-state relationships affirms the legitimate secular character of the state, but clearly expects that the church should cooperate with secular authorities in areas touching the human dignity and human rights of the person. The international structure and polity of Catholicism is reasserted in terms of those characteristics (hierarchical, sacramental, institutional) that Troeltsch described as essential for the church-type.

Lines of continuity are clear, but there are some differences. The church-type expectation of society involves a mix of conflict and cooperation. There are indications in Vatican II's teaching that the potential for conflict between church and state or church and society is high. The expectation of differences with the wider society and tension between the church and major institutions in society does not preclude a church-type presence in society, but it does signal that there will be pressure on the church-type model from external factors and from groups within the church seeking a more radical differentiation of the "two cities." As Troeltsch might have expected, the arena of modern warfare provides one of the most likely points of contestation between church and society.

THE CHURCH AND THE WORLD IN
THE NUCLEAR AGE

The decisive impact of the *Pastoral Constitution* on the pastoral letter was both ecclesiological and moral. *The Challenge of Peace* goes beyond the conciliar analysis of nuclear warfare, but it is rooted in the Council's conception of the challenge posed by modern war.

The Council as the Catalyst for
the Pastoral Letter

Both the tone and the themes of Vatican II's teaching on the nuclear age illustrate the stress placed on a church-type ethic by this new mode of war. The historical link between Roman Catholic ecclesiology and its just-war ethic has been one of the prime characteristics of the church-type model. The church both affirmed the right of political authority to use force in defense of the community and simultaneously sought to limit the kind of force used.

The *Pastoral Constitution* acknowledged the state's right to use force as a last resort in the world governed by sovereign states and devoid of a centralized political authority. But much of the chapter on war was devoted to highlighting the difficulty of meeting the traditional criteria of limitation in the era of modern warfare. From the opening of the chapter, the tone is one of extreme urgency and a sense of moral crisis:

> The development of armaments by modern science has immeasurably magnified the horrors and wickedness of war. Warfare conducted with these weapons can inflict immense and indiscriminate havoc which goes far beyond the bounds of legitimate defense.[7]

The tone of urgency pervades the substance of the analysis in the *Pastoral Constitution*. The conciliar text contains three themes that shaped the pastoral letter. First, it acknowledged and legitimated the witness of nonviolence in a world marked by multiple forms of violence. Second, it reaffirmed the continuing validity of just-war concepts by using them to set definite limits on permissible uses of force. Third, it took note of the paradoxical quality of deterrence and it initiated (but did not conclude) an assessment of the morality of stockpiling and threatening to use nuclear weapons.

The conciliar chapter on war was a remarkable step forward in Catholic teaching but it was not a finished product. Its value resided in its catalytic character far more than in its conclusions. It called the church "to undertake a completely fresh reappraisal of war."[8] And it put the world on notice that a church-type ethic did not mean that all of the modern state's preparations for war would be morally acceptable.

The Pastoral Letter: The Moral Argument

The *Challenge of Peace* stands in the line of the *Pastoral Constitution;* it is essentially a just-war analysis of the nuclear age. To compare the two documents is to feel the twenty years of changing technology and strategy that stand between them. None of the dangers described by the Council has subsided; indeed the capacity for destruction has increased both quantitatively and qualitatively. The moral limits of tolerance for resort to force were approached in the *Pastoral Constitution;* they are pressed to the breaking point in the pastoral letter.

The U.S. Bishops pressed the just-war analysis to a greater degree of specificity and technical detail than the Council attempted. The results of this specific testing of the meaning of nuclear war can be summarized in terms of the premise of the moral argument, the assessment of three cases of use of nuclear weapons, and the analysis of deterrence.

The premise of the bishops' just-war analysis is that limitation of the use of force means addressing the question of whether nuclear weapons can be controlled at any level of use. The issue of control was a major theme in the preparation of the several drafts of the pastoral letter, in the literature consulted, and in the extensive dialogues the bishops' drafting committee (Cardinal Bernardin's committee) had with the Reagan administration.

The result of this detailed process of research and discussion was an attitude in the letter that is radically skeptical about the possibilities of controlling nuclear war. The pastoral stands in the line of the strategic theorists who stress the drastic discontinuity of nuclear and conventional weapons. Because of their profound skepticism about control, the bishops say no to the idea of nuclear war, and set themselves against the careless rhetoric used at times about "winnable" nuclear wars or "prevailing" in nuclear war. Against this pattern of thought the bishops seek to build a political-moral barrier against any use of nuclear weapons and to resist the rhetoric that would lead us toward use.

The pastoral letter comments on *three cases of use* of nuclear weapons. The first case is directly intended attacks on civilian populations or "Counter-Population Warfare." This case is considered for two reasons: (1) the moral principle at stake, noncombatant immunity, is central to the just-war ethic; and (2) at various times in the nuclear age the direct targeting of civilian centers has been considered or planned. The basic judgment of the letter is to rule out, absolutely, direct attacks on civilian populations. The judgment is based upon the just-war tradition which found forceful expression in the Second Vatican Council's statement against "destruction of entire cities or of extensive areas along with their population. . . . It merits unequivocal and unhesitating condemnation."[9]

The second case, "The Initiation of Nuclear War," is the question of first use of nuclear weapons. The significance of this issue is twofold—the possibility of "first use" is still a central piece of NATO strategy and a renewed debate about the strategy is now under way. The bishops do not address the political debate as such; their purpose is to isolate the moral question in it. Briefly stated, is there a specific moral issue involved in the willingness to be the first party to move warfare from the conventional level to the nuclear level?

The pastoral finds a specific moral responsibility here and its judgment is one of the more controversial sections of the letter. The bishops say: "We do not perceive any situation in which the deliberate initiation of nuclear warfare, on however restricted a scale, can be morally justified. Non-nuclear attacks by another state must be resisted by other than nuclear means. Therefore, a serious moral obligation exists to develop non-nuclear defensive strategies as rapidly as possible."[10]

The rationale of the pastoral's prohibition of first use should be seen in light of a general theme of the letter. In a series of judgments the bishops seek to build a multidimensional barrier against resort to nuclear weapons, to insulate them, as much as possible, from quick, early, or easy use. The specific support the bishops give to a "no first use" position should be seen as a dimension of this larger theme in the letter.

The third case is "Limited Nuclear War." Here again the bishops enter, as we have seen, a much-disputed technical question with a long history in the strategic and ethical literature. They are aware that they cannot "settle" the empirical debate of whether a limited nuclear exchange can be kept "limited." Their approach in the pastoral is to raise a series of moral and empirical questions that express their radical skepticism about controlling such an exchange. Having pressed the question of what "limited" really means, they make the following assessment: "One of the criteria of the just-war tradition is a reasonable hope of success in bringing about justice and peace. We must ask whether such a reasonable hope can exist once nuclear weapons have been exchanged. The burden of proof remains on those who assert that meaningful limitation is possible."[11] In light of this intricate position on use the bishops address *the strategy of deterrence.* Religious-moral analysis does not dissolve the formidable empirical challenge posed by deterrence. The paradox of deterrence was captured by a phrase used by the Second Vatican Council: "the stockpiling of arms which grows from year-to-year serves, in a way hitherto unthought of, as a deterrent to potential attackers. Many people look upon this as the most effective way known at the present time for maintaining some sort of peace among nations."[12]

Embedded in this cryptic description is an acknowledgment of the new reality posed by deterrence. The result of deterrence, "some sort of peace," is described here in language meant to convey the unsatisfactory basis of our present security. The difficult political and moral issue is whether any other available means would even preserve a "sort of peace." Not specified in Vatican II's early and brief analysis of the problem of deterrence are the following questions which have structured the postconciliar analysis of deterrence.

- Does effective deterrence involve a "formed intention" to do evil?
- How should the relationship of threat, intention, and possible use be related?
- How do we weigh morally the argument that deterrence has served the function of preventing any use of nuclear weapons?
- Would less reliance on nuclear deterrence have the effect of "making the world safe for conventional war"?

The U. S. Bishops' position, rooted in Vatican II but pushed beyond the conciliar judgment, was a carefully phrased conditional acceptance of deterrence:

> These considerations of concrete elements of nuclear deterrence policy, made in light of John Paul II's evaluation, but applying it through our own prudential judgments, lead us to a strictly conditioned moral acceptance of nuclear deterrence. We cannot consider it adequate as a long-term basis for peace.[13]

Devoid of all modifiers, the judgment on deterrence is "acceptance" not "condemnation." But the acceptance is "strictly conditioned"; this phrase places two kinds of restraint on the strategy of deterrence. The first is "temporal" in nature; both John Paul II and the American bishops tie the justification for deterrence to an understanding that it be used as a framework for moving to a different basis of security among nations. This temporal assessment means that the "direction" of deterrence policy has moral significance—are steps being taken to move away from this fragile, paradoxical basis for interstate relations or is the direction of policy simply reinforcing the present state of affairs?

The second restraint concerns the "character" of the deterrent. The strictly conditioned justification of the deterrent rests upon its role of "preventing the use of nuclear weapons or other actions which could lead directly to a nuclear exchange.[14] The point here is to limit the role of nuclear deterrence to a very specific function in world affairs; the posture of deterrence is not to be used to pursue goals other than preventing nuclear war.

My purpose in making this detailed assessment of the pastoral letter's evaluation of nuclear weapons is to illustrate how the letter went beyond the

Pastoral Constitution but remained within the church-type analysis of war. The judgments made on first-use, limited nuclear war and the strategy of deterrence all were more detailed, more technical in character, and more stringent in substance than the Second Vatican Council had been.

Yet different specific moral judgment did not mean a different ecclesial style than the conciliar text. In the years after the Council some had argued that the just-war ethic was no longer relevant or useful in assessing the challenges of nuclear war. Many echoed James Douglass's comment:

> The state of just-war doctrine in contemporary Catholic thought is roughly equivalent to that of the prohibition against contraception: it has lost its cogency in terms of current theological thought and continues in use primarily as a point of reference for those who wish to go beyond it. [15]

The U.S. Bishops took a different position: they affirmed the continuing value of the just-war principles and sought to illustrate their relevance by using them to rule out many of the ideas and proposals that had shaped the nuclear debate. The ancient ethic as the pastoral letter applied it made the U.S. Bishops very severe critics of existing policy.

It is important to note, however, that the stringent moral critique of nuclear policy found in the letter did not lead the bishops to advocate a sectarian break with the state or society. A deep difference of perspective and policy had surfaced with the publication of the pastoral, but the bishops reaffirmed the conviction of the *Pastoral Constitution* that the church fulfilled its ministry to the world by staying in sustained dialogue with the world. [16]

The Pastoral Letter:
The Ecclesiological Argument

To understand the position of the pastoral letter in its determination to remain in dialogue with the major institutions of society while holding a moral position that runs counter to existing policy, it is necessary to locate the bishops' letter in a larger Catholic debate that had followed the Vatican Council. The pastoral letter did not identify with either of the two positions that were in the postconciliar debate.

The first was a collage of specific positions that did not fit securely either in a just-war argument or the church-type ethic. Although these positions originated as *moral* assessments of the nuclear age, they contained ecclesiological implications. The more profoundly they drew the comparison between the Christian ethic of war and the policies of nuclear nations, the more difficult it became to sustain the church-type posture toward the state.

The dynamic that related these positions was a movement toward a non-violent option in the Catholic community. The movement arose in three stages. First, in the 1960s a position of nuclear pacifism surfaced in response to nuclear deterrence strategy. The principal arguments for this position were found in England, among Catholic philosophers who all held the just-war ethic but were convinced that nuclear weapons could not be contained within the just-war criteria.[17]

Second, in the United States the Vietnam War galvanized a number of Catholics to affirm a position going beyond nuclear pacifism. The writings of Gordon Zahn, Daniel Berrigan, and Thomas Merton, while differing in details, approximated a classical nonviolent position.[18]

Third, in the 1970s the rapid growth of the *Pax Christi* movement among bishops, priests, and laity produced a constituency that emphasized nonviolence as the distinctive Christian contribution to any discussion of war and peace.[19]

It would be forcing the evidence to say that a single ecclesiological vision could be traced through this process of development. The focus was on the *moral* response to modern war and ecclesiological questions were raised only implicitly. The English nuclear pacifists and Zahn assumed the church-type ethic and tried to fuse it with a new moral position on warfare. The position of Berrigan and some representatives of *Pax Christi* did connect the new critique of war with a call for a reevaluation of the church's relationship to the wider society. Would any of the three positions advocate a "sect-type" ecclesiology? Not in Troeltsch's terms, but some of these representatives would clearly see a sectarian distance from society as implied by the differences they perceived between the Christian view of life and the likely requirements of fighting a modern war.

The push toward nonviolence and separation from the prevailing public policy was not the only force in the ecclesial debate. Throughout the drafting process, Catholic variants of the Christian realist position were proposed. In different ways both Michael Novak and William O'Brien spoke for the realist position.[20] In contrast to the Merton-Zahn position, which would rule out both the use of nuclear weapons and the strategy of deterrence, the realist case sought to contain but not to condemn the central features of nuclear strategy. Ecclesiologically, the realist position places a significant responsibility on the church to develop moral positions that take into consideration in an explicit way the nature of the Soviet threat to the West. This requirement, acknowledged by others but not with the same weight, stresses the degree to which the realists see the church as part of the larger society and responsible for it.

The Challenge of Peace reflects the differences that had developed in

Catholicism since the Vatican Council, but it also stakes out its own position. The ecclesiological themes are found in chapters 1 and 4 of the pastoral. It is possible to distinguish a dominant church-type ecclesiological posture in the document from subordinate themes which illustrate the moral tension in the church-society relationship under the conditions of the nuclear age.

Two characteristics of the ecclesiological section place the pastoral securely in a church-type model: its conception of the public role of the church and its style of teaching.

The pastoral letter conveys a strong sense of the church's public role. This is expressed in terms of ecclesial responsibility to be present in the nuclear debate. The bishops ground this responsibility in the teaching ministry of the church and the fact that they are called to teach in one of the two major nuclear nations:

> In this pastoral letter we speak as bishops of the universal Church, heirs of the religious and moral teaching on modern warfare of the last four decades. We also speak as bishops of the Church in the United States, who have both the obligation and the opportunity to share and interpret the moral and religious wisdom of the Catholic tradition by applying it to the problems of war and peace today.[21]

There is a double conviction reflected in this passage and in the pastoral as a whole. First, there is a strong sense that the nature of the nuclear-arms race presents such a challenge to the traditional moral teaching that failure to address the issue imperils the moral fiber of the Catholic tradition. Second, there is a sense that the moral categories, if brought into the public debate, can illuminate both the personal and policy choices that we face in the nuclear age.

The ecclesiological posture of this statement is that of a "public church";[22] the nuclear issue is a wider concern than that of Christians or believers. It is described as a "cosmic drama" in which one serious mistake could have global consequences. The public posture of the church involves both a sense of responsibility for the welfare of the whole society and a recognition that the church must make common cause with others (scientists, politicians, scholars) if the nuclear threat is to be confronted adequately. The perspective of the pastoral is that there is a specifically moral-religious contribution to be made to the nuclear dilemma, but the problem will not yield to an exclusively moral-religious approach. The church of the pastoral letter is "public" in the sense that it consciously accepts public responsibility in the policy debate and it enters the public debate as one participant among others.

This public sense of ministry is made clear in the way the bishops define the purposes of the pastoral letter:

Catholic teaching on peace and war has had two purposes: to help Catholics form their consciences and to contribute to the public policy debate about the morality of war.[23]

This statement touches both the role of the church in the public debate and the style of the church's teaching. Stanley Hauerwas has argued that the social ethic of the church should be directed to the church—its purpose is to shape Christian witness over against society.[24] The pastoral letter, reflecting a classic church-type position, defines the role of social teaching differently. There is a pastoral purpose directed toward the community of the church, but also a public role projecting the ecclesial position into the wider secular arena.

This dual role for Catholic social teaching requires a specific style of presentation. As the pastoral observes, "The conviction, rooted in Catholic ecclesiology, that both the community of the faithful and the civil community should be addressed on peace and war has produced two complementary but distinct styles of teaching."[25] The pastoral letter describes these two styles in terms of an approach that emphasizes "the problems and requirements of a just public policy," and in terms of another approach that emphasizes "the specific role which Christians should play" in witnessing to the gospel.[26]

In this discussion of the church's public role and its mode of teaching on social questions, the pastoral again reflects continuity with Catholic tradition as well as changes within that tradition since Vatican II. Troeltsch and others have noted that much of Catholic social teaching has been primarily philosophical rather than theological. The church's sense of its public role and its responsibility to shape the wider life of society led it to use philosophical and secular concepts to express its views on social questions. The twofold rationale for this joining of philosophical with theological reasoning has been that the evangelical teaching of the Scriptures does not, by itself, provide sufficient guidance for complex social questions, and the arguments for a given social position need to be expressed in terms that are open to forging alliances of believers and nonbelievers in support of centrally important social values.

The papal social encyclicals from Leo XIII through John XXIII exemplified this strongly philosophical mode of teaching as did Catholic medical and sexual ethics. The just-war ethic was perhaps the most well-known example of a "Catholic teaching" which in fact was rooted in pre-Christian

Stoic philosophy and has been used extensively outside the Catholic tradition.

One of the major developments in Catholic moral teaching since the 1960s has been a reemphasis on the role of the Scriptures, a more explicit appeal to the centrally Christian sources of moral insight. The shift from a philosophical to a biblical-theological style is best seen by comparing John XXIII's encyclical *Peace on Earth* (1963) with Vatican II's *Pastoral Constitution* (1965). While chronologically very close the two documents are qualitatively different in their mode of analysis. The encyclical represents the natural-law social ethic in one of its most systematic expressions in Catholic teaching. The *Pastoral Constitution* is clearly not antiphilosophical but is known principally for its evangelical-theological tone and style.

When addressing the morality of war, the difference in the two styles becomes particularly pronounced. The just-war tradition in Catholic teaching has always had a *theological grounding* (e.g., Augustine's theological anthropology preceded his discussion of war; Aquinas treated war in his analysis of the virtue of charity), but it is a refined *philosophical expression* filled with distinctions and complex modes of moral reasoning. The more biblically based treatment of warfare has often produced a mode of pacifist witness, sharper in its condemnation of war and less likely to weigh conflicting claims that could lead to justifying some use of force. Not surprisingly, the emergence of a nonviolent position within Catholicism was tied to some degree to a more explicitly evangelical interpretation of the problem of warfare.

The pastoral letter explicitly refers to "the range of strongly held opinion in the Catholic community on war and peace,"[27] and it makes a serious effort to reflect these views within the framework of a coherent position.

The pastoral begins with an extensive biblical reflection on war and peace; it acknowledges the emergence of the nonviolent position in the Catholic community and it affirms the legitimacy of such a position for an individual. The crucial analytical move, however, is the pastoral's reassertion of the just-war ethic as the public position of the church on warfare.[28]

This endorsement of the just-war position is critically important ecclesiologically because it signals a continuation of the ecclesiological-moral posture that has characterized the church-type. The entire tone and analysis of the pastoral letter is designed to illustrate that the continuance of a just-war position is *barely* possible in the nuclear age. This makes all the more significant, however, the structural continuity which can be illustrated by the "public church" and just-war affirmations found in *The Challenge of Peace*.

The continuity is never simply a reassertion of the church-type described by Troeltsch. Both the external challenge posed by modern warfare and the internal changes in Catholic theology find expression in the final section of the letter where the bishops offer pastoral advice to Catholics. Here some of the stress on the church-type posture is sensed. The section on discipleship notes that "It is clear today, perhaps more than in previous generations that convinced Christians are a minority in nearly every country of the world—including nominally Christian and Catholic nations. . . . As believers we can identify rather easily with the early Church as a company of witnesses engaged in a difficult mission."[29]

The tone of this description does not fit a traditional church-type conception of the status of disciples. The stress on minority status and the acceptance of a significant difference between the Christian conception of life and prevailing cultural standards raise questions about the logic of the church-type posture of the pastoral. It is useful, I believe, to distinguish between the structural presence of the church in society and the existential conditions in which Christians live.

The traditional church-type model presupposed both a "Christian culture" for which the church was responsible and a majority of Christians in the population. The pastoral letter affirms a public responsibility for the church, conveys a strong sense of the bishops' conviction that the church should play a public moral role, but does not imply either an expectation of a numerically Christian society or a presumption that Christians will be often reinforced by the prevailing values of our culture. The pastoral presumes instead that the church should play a public role in a secular context; it will be a minority church but it cannot forsake a public role.

This prescription is reflected in the section of the pastoral where Christians in diverse vocations are offered guidance. The tenor and themes of the guidance stress active participation in society as citizens. It presumes Catholics will be in public affairs, in the military, and in the scientific and defense communities. The letter stresses the stringency of the choices individuals will face, but its general orientation is a church-type witness in and through the diverse vocations that constitute contemporary society. For both individuals and institutions the pastoral letter envisions church-type witness under new conditions.

CATHOLIC POSTURE AND THE CHURCH-TYPE—
THE U.S. BISHOPS

If one looks beyond the topic of war and peace, the linkage between the Catholic style and the church-type model is intensified. By the mid-1980s the Catholic bishops were deeply and publicly involved in four major policy debates in the United States: (1) abortion, (2) the nuclear question, (3) U.S. policy in Central America, and (4) social justice and the economy. This is not the place to analyze the specific positions the bishops have taken on each question; it is rather the time to look at the character of their participation in the policy debates.

The presence of the bishops in the public-policy debate is shaped by the theology of Vatican II and the experience of ministering in a pluralistic democracy. The Council, as we have seen, provided a theology that affirmed the secular status of the state, acknowledged the separation of church and state, and called for an activist church presence in the life of society. In a series of major addresses in the 1980s key spokesmen for the U.S. Bishops have adapted the conciliar vision to the specific conditions of political life in this local church.

Three of these speeches, by Cardinal Joseph Bernardin, Archbishop John R. Roach, and Bishop James A. Malone,[30] have set forth a contemporary Catholic understanding of the role of religion in public affairs and the specific place of a "public church" in light of the American constitutional system. While supporting the principle of the separation of church and state in the First Amendment, the three bishops set limits to the separation principle lest it be used to argue for the separation of the church from society or religion from culture. As Cardinal Bernardin, commenting on the work of John Courtney Murray, put the case:

> The purpose of the First Amendment, Murray taught us, was not to silence the religious voice but to free religion from state control so that moral-religious values and principles could be taught and cultivated in the wider society. . . . The goal of the American system is to provide space for a religious substance in society but not a religious state.[31]

Historically, the church-type has usually tried to provide religious substance in society precisely through the instrumentality of a religious state. The theology of Vatican II and the convictions of the U.S. Bishops join in an affirmation that such a model is neither possible nor desirable today. The refusal of a religious role for the state does not mean the abdication of a public role for the church. The theology that guides the bishops is less political in a church-state sense (it expects less explicit help from the state) but more political in a church-society understanding of the church's ministry. The premises of that ministry—responsibility for the structure of social institutions as well as the character of individuals, sensitivity to the social consequences of issues, a search for common ground with other social actors—all fit the church-type model. Bishop Malone caught the spirit of this theology of social ministry in this 1984 Presidential Address to the Bishops' Conference:

> A useful place to begin is simply to locate the position the Catholic Bishops hold in the public arena . . . both our theological tradition and our organizational structure provide the Catholic Church with specific resources to contribute to the wider civil and religious discussion . . . the social nature of Catholicism makes it particularly sensitive to the social significance of issues and provides us with the capacity to address the other major social institutions of society.[32]

Revising the church-type without rejecting its premises about the church's social presence has forced a rethinking of how the church influences the wider culture. The rethinking has been produced by theological change within the church and by responding to the specific challenge of a pluralist democracy. Theologically, the shift which occurred between Leo XIII and Pius XII in Catholic teaching on church and state prepared for the revision of the church-type. Murray analyzed the change from considering, as Leo XIII did, the citizen as the *object* of the responsibility of both church and state to Pius XII's conceptions of the citizen as the *subject* of the refashioning of every social system.[33] Leo XIII's conception fostered an authoritarian conception of governance and social change; institutions acted *for* people. Pius XII, in his social theory at least, has a strong sense of the citizen as the agent *through whom* the church should work for change and the one *to whom* the state should answer.

This perspective provides a method for the exercise of the church's public ministry. The notion that the church deals less directly with the state but more extensively with citizens who can both address their state and shape their society corresponds to Vatican II's principle of the freedom of the church. The one requirement the church needs in society is the freedom to preach, teach, and organize its constituency. Bishop Malone described the dynamics of the method as the church working at the intersection of public opinion and public policy. The possibilities of this model of public ministry were highlighted in a statement of John Paul II which the bishops used in the peace pastoral:

> Peace cannot be built by the power of rulers alone. Peace can be firmly constructed only if it corresponds to the resolute determination of all people of good will. Rulers must be supported and enlightened by a public opinion that encourages them or, where necessary, expresses disapproval.[34]

This conception that public opinion is a significant arena for the church's ministry requires further analysis in terms of two questions: how public opinion relates to public policy, and how the church should relate to public opinion. In a constitutional democracy the impact of public opinion on policy is both significant and complicated. Public opinion hardly ever dictates specific policy choices but it does set a definable atmosphere within which people make choices, and it can draw some key lines beyond which democratically elected leaders can move only at substantial risk. In recent history the role of public opinion was demonstrable as a positive force in civil rights and in the resistance it created to carrying on the war in Vietnam. But public opinion does not guarantee a specific outcome; at times it does not send a clear message and at other times it takes too long to shape opinion on an issue.

The church, therefore, has an "indirect" impact on policy when working through the medium of public opinion. By choosing this method of influence, however, the church stays clearly within its area of competency. The task of shaping public opinion is an extension of the church's teaching ministry. The teaching ministry is exercised on the two levels outlined earlier in this chapter. The church addresses its own community and it also enters the wider public debate as a major social institution. At both levels of argument the bishops have tried to highlight and sharpen the moral dimensions of the public argument on the issues of abortion, human rights, nuclear strategy, and the economy.

On all four issues the style of participation has fit a church-type model. The decision to seek a constitutional amendment to reverse the Supreme Court's 1973 decisions on abortion expresses a commitment to shape the wider culture on the abortion question, not simply to protect Catholics from the culture. Similarly, on the nuclear question, the pastoral letter sought to shape the policy debate as a whole not simply to provide guidance for discipleship in individual cases.

A key characteristic of sustaining this revised church-type model (i.e., acting like a church but without help from the state, and devoid of majority support in the population) is the criteria by which church participation in the public debate will be assessed. Bishop Malone stated the case clearly:

> In the public arena of a pluralistic democracy religious leaders face the same tests of rational argument as any other individuals or institutions. Our impact on the public will be directly proportionate to the persuasiveness of our positions. We seek no special status and we should not be accorded one.[35]

To meet these "tests of rational argument" the church faces two distinct tasks. First, there is the challenge of rendering a religiously grounded moral vision accessible to a wider public. In a Catholic version of the church-type this task has always been understood as part of public ministry. The bishops have sustained this style, seeking on all four issues to account for their position in terms that a pluralistic public will find convincing. Second, the standards of "rational argument" require a specific level of competency in relating moral insight to the complex empirical character of public issues. The detailed character of the pastoral letters on the nuclear question and the economy illustrate the effort required to join the ethical and empirical arguments in public debate.

On all four issues the U.S. Bishops have addressed, there is a constant pull to move away from the church-type model toward either a more passive, nonpolitical position or toward a more confrontational, prophetic posture. The argument for passivity runs counter to the general postconciliar direction of Catholic social teaching and pastoral leadership; it is not having a major impact at present in the Catholic community.

The case for a more radical break with prevailing public attitudes can come either from the ecclesiastical "left" or "right," and both sides have made their case in the 1980s. At times those opposing abortion see the present situation requiring a posture of total confrontation with American society—or of withdrawal from it. A similar case is made—usually by different people—on the nuclear question. Cardinal Bernardin, who has served as chairman of both the pastoral on peace and the episcopal committee addressing the abortion issue, and has heard the argument for a "sectarian" posture on both issues, stated his views in terms which characterize the general thrust of the U.S. Bishops' position on public questions:

> Despite the radical moral skepticism of the pastoral letter about ever containing the use of nuclear weapons within justifiable limits, the bishops were not persuaded that this moral judgment should lead to an ecclesial posture of withdrawal from dialogue or participation in the public life of the nation. Rather, in accord with the traditional Catholic conception, they affirmed a posture of dialogue with the secular world. I am the first to say—after the past three years—that it is a precarious posture, but one I find more adequate than either total silence within society or absolute separation from society.[36]

The quotation provides a response to the question raised at the outset of this chapter. The Roman Catholic Church has not fundamentally changed its moral and ecclesial vision from a church-type model. But it has found it necessary to revise the content of the church-type theology of church and state and to recast its conception of how to fulfill a public role in society. The forces requiring these changes have been a mix of internal theological assessment and external issues that pose substantially new challenges to some traditional moral categories. The church-type remains visible in Catholicism but it exists in a new context and with new content.

NOTES

1. Ernst Troeltsch (1869-1923), German Protestant theologian and historian, developed a classic threefold typology of the social embodiments of the Christian faith: *Kirche* or church ("an institution endowed with grace and salvation"); *Sekte* or sect ("a voluntary society, composed of strict and definite Christian believers"); and *Mystik* or mysticism ("a purely personal and inward experience"). All three modes, Troeltsch held, derive from the gospel. Thus the second and third, like the first, are sui generis, and not mere deformations. (Ed.)

2. National Conference of Catholic Bishops, *The Challenge of Peace: God's Promise and Our Response* (Washington, D.C.: U.S. Catholic Conference, 1983); hereafter cited as *C.P.* with relevant paragraph and page numbers.

3. *C.P.*, #7, pp. 3-4.

4. Both texts are found in A. Flannery, O.P., ed., *Vatican Council II: The Conciliar and Post-Conciliar Documents* (Collegeville, Minn.: The Liturgical Press, 1975). *The Pastoral Constitution on the Church in the Modern World*, hereafter cited as *The Pastoral Constitution* with paragraph and page numbers; and *The Declaration on Religious Liberty*, cited with paragraph and page numbers.

5. Cf. J. C. Murray, S.J., "The Problem of Religious Freedom," *Theological Studies* 25 (1964): 503-75, esp. 507-12.

6. *The Pastoral Constitution*, #40, p. 940.

7. Ibid., #80, p. 989.

8. Ibid.

9. Ibid., p. 990.

10. *C.P.*, #150, p. 47.

11. Ibid., #159, p. 50.

12. *The Pastoral Constitution*, #81, p. 990.

13. *C.P.*, #186, p. 58.

14. Ibid., #185, p. 58.

15. J. Douglass, *The Nonviolent Cross: A Theology of Revolution and Peace* (New York: Macmillan Co., 1966), 155.

16. *The Pastoral Constitution*, #3, p. 904; cf. *C.P.*, #3, pp. 1-2; #16-17, pp. 6-7; #21, p. 8.

17. W. Stein, ed., *Nuclear Weapons and the Christian Conscience* (London: Merlin Press, 1961).

18. Cf. G. C. Zahn, *War, Conscience and Dissent* (New York: Hawthorn, 1967); T. Merton, *Faith and Violence: Christian Teaching and Christian Practice* (Notre Dame, Ind.: University of Notre Dame Press, 1968); cf. articles by J. Fahey, "Pax Christi," S. Lammers, "Roman Catholic Social Ethics and Pacifism," in *War or Peace? The Search for New Answers*, ed. T. Shannon (New York: Orbis Books, 1980).

19. See Shannon, *War or Peace?*; also G. C. Zahn, "Pacifism and Just War," in *Catholics and Nuclear War*, ed. P. Murnion (New York: Crossroad, 1983), 119-31.

20. M. Novak, *Moral Clarity in the Nuclear Age* (Nashville: Thomas Nelson, 1983); W. O'Brien, "The Challenge of War: A Christian Realist Perspective," in *The Catholic Bishops and Nuclear War*, ed. J. A. Dwyer, S.S.J. (Washington, D.C.: Georgetown University Press, 1984), 37-64.

21. *C.P.*, #5, p. 3.

22. The phrase has been used systematically in M. Marty, *The Public Church* (New York: Crossroad, 1981).

23. *C.P.*. #16, p. 6.

24. S. Hauerwas, *A Community of Character: Toward A Constructive Christian Ethic* (Notre Dame, Ind.: University of Notre Dame Press, 1981), 1-2, 90-94.

25. *C.P.*, #17, p. 7.

26. Ibid., #18, p. 7.

27. Ibid., #12, p. 5.

28. Ibid., #75, p. 24.

29. Ibid., #276, p. 86.

30. Cardinal Bernardin, "Religion and Politics: The Future Agenda," *Origins* 14 (1984): 323ff.; Archbishop Roach, "The Need for Public Dialogue on Religion and Politics," *Origins* 11 (1981): 391ff.; Bishop Malone, "Intersection of Public Opinion and Public Policy," *Origins* 14 (1984): 386ff.

31. Bernardin, "Religion and Politics," 323.

32. Malone, "Intersection of Public Opinion and Public Policy," 386, 387.

33. Murray, "The Problem of Religious Freedom."

34. John Paul II, "World Day of Peace Message 1982," *Origins* 11 (1982): 477.

35. Malone, "Intersection of Public Opinion and Public Policy," 386.

36. Cardinal Bernardin, "The Church in the Public Life of the Nation," *Origins* 13 (1984): 567.

II

PEACE-WAR POSITIONS NEWLY STATED

4

FORGIVEN VIOLENCE: CHRISTIAN RESPONSIBILITY BETWEEN PACIFISM AND JUST WAR

CHARLES C. WEST

It is appropriate to begin with words from a practitioner of war: "There is many a boy here today who looks on war as all glory, but boys, it is all hell." So William Tecumseh Sherman, the devastator of Georgia, addressed a convention of Civil War veterans in 1880. Public memory has shortened his wisdom to the pungent bit of negative theology: "War is hell."

The language is of course symbolic. There is a lot more to hell than even thermonuclear catastrophe can encompass. There are other demons abroad in the world than war—tyranny, torture, terrorism, and economic oppression to name only a few. The traditional four horsemen of the apocalypse—War, Famine, Pestilence, and Death—have become a mechanized rabble. They surround us on all sides and work in our midst. We can hardly avoid choosing some to fight others, then having to repent of our choice at the next stage of the struggle. War is not the only devil. Yet something is said about it in General Sherman's phrase which, as our mood swings between managerial confidence and desperate protest, we tend to forget. War is, like hell, unlimited. Once in it we lose our footing and are swept along by its tide. War is compelling. We are caught in its forces despite ourselves. This is the context in which we must exercise our responsibility and make our witness.

War, like hell, is in its nature *unlimited*. To kill other people is an ultimate, irreversible act. Such an act, even in legally defensible forms such as self-defense or capital punishment, raises moral questions, but war goes

---

Charles C. West is Stephen Colwell Professor of Christian Ethics, and past Dean, Princeton Theological Seminary. He has served in China and Europe under the United Presbyterian Church, and as Associate Director of the Ecumenical Institute in Bossey, Switzerland.

further. War is the organization of brute power by a political body to break whatever system of law and order controlled that body's relations with others to make another more to its liking. It does deliberate violence to the balance of interests and influences through which nations and peoples normally seek their own well-being and further their interests while accepting the limits posed by the needs and desires of others. It smashes the order, the consensus, or the contract by which society had lived before, and tears open the network of relationships which society had called its peace. It is, in its essence, a *transgression of limits*. The party that makes war recognizes therefore no other limits than its own definition of what is just and good, or the superior power of opposing forces.

There have been limited wars. Wars are certainly limited in the intention of most warmakers. Augustine's observation nearly sixteen hundred years ago that no one makes war for its own sake, but only to achieve a more desirable peace, still holds true. When the peace sought is modest enough—repulsion of an invasion, for example, or a relative advantage in wealth or politics—a successful war may be limited in conduct as well. The last forty years are full of examples: China's almost-forgotten invasion of India, Israel's various encounters with its neighbors, and the recent affair of the Falkland Islands, to name only three. And even when war aims surpass all limits—"to make the world safe for democracy," "to crush the power of international Communism," or "to liberate the people of the world from their oppressors"—subtle forces operate to undermine their boundless dynamic from within. Success breeds cynicism about all great causes for which people kill. The Crusades are an early example. The First World War is another. The moral tension of a belligerent ideal grows slack when the enemy is found within as well as without. Pragmatic accommodation begins to take over. One can cite today's China as evidence.

Furthermore, outside forces, though they may not prevent war altogether, do sometimes contain the warmaker's power in some acceptable larger order. The Catholic Church had some success in medieval Europe with its just-war criteria whenever dukes and kings believed that the divine order the church expressed controlled their destinies in time and in eternity. Today the structures of order claim less ultimacy and their laws are less definite but they still work sometimes. The United Nations has provided the context for limiting war in Korea, in Zaire, and at times on the borders of Israel. The awful reality of a balance of nuclear arms continually limits the intervention of one great power in the sphere of influence of the other. War is limited today by an almost metaphysical fear of what would happen if just causes were allowed the full fury of their natural bent, or the drive for security were made absolute. Wars can be limited, by shrewd self-interest in a context of international relations, by disillusioned cynicism, or by fear of terrible costs and consequences, even if no longer by fear of divine judgment. "Der liebe Gott," as Einstein said in another context, "ist raffiniert" ("The good God is clever"). Or, as the psalmist put it, "Surely the wrath of men shall praise thee" (76:10a).

There are problems, however, with making these factors into a method for domesticating and justifying war. First, they are all external to the nature and logic of the act of war itself. Indeed they seem to contradict whatever justice lay in the cause that provoked the war in the first place. Compromise is inherently unsatisfying; disillusion cries out for reinspiration. The warmaker who started out to change the order of relationships by violence may be restrained by calculating consequences but he or she will not accept the situation as order. The seeds of war lie fallow when they do not bloom in victory, waiting for a change in climate.

Second, the factors that limit war are inherently unstable, both those which concern its cause and those which concern its conduct. The reasons for going to war are always set forth in terms that seem just to the perpetrator. Appeal to the public opinion of humanity, even to that of the enemy, is common. But no rebuttal is invited. The act of war breaks off dialogue. In moving to violence the warmaker disrupts the structures that would subject his or her argument to any higher court. There may be a degree of justice in the cause, but there is never as much as he or she imagines, and there is no longer any way of preventing his or her relative justice from being made absolute. The warmaker is enclosed in a self-justifying ideology for which there is no effective correction. This then affects the conduct of the war. Even relatively just violence, discriminating in its targets and proportional to the victory and new peace it aims to achieve, is brutal and unjust toward some who experience its secondary effects as primary. But there is no tribunal to which the injured can go. There is no enforcement of *jus in bello*, save fear of reprisal (which does, to some degree, protect prisoners), and no definitions that work, save those of the belligerents. The final dynamic in a war situation that moves toward the bursting of all limits is fear of defeat, fear of losing control of one's political, social, and even moral autonomy, which makes the goal of victory justify all actions.

This is the problem with all attempts to define a just use of violence, in war or in revolution. No earthly power exists that can define such justice authoritatively and limit war effectively according to it. None is free enough of interested bias to render objective judgment. None is strong enough to enforce its biased authority regardless. The struggle in the world is for the power to determine what shall and shall not be called just, and to enforce that determination. The demand for justice incites conflict; it does not limit it. Such peace as the world enjoys is the result of compromise among powers who have less to lose by maintaining the present order than by upsetting it—a compromise constantly called in question by those who have too little power and too little justice to find the order worth respecting.

War is unlimited. It is also *compelling*. This is partly because there are organized groups of people in the world, who will resort to violence to pursue their interests or enforce their ideals, against whom we must defend ourselves. There are, to be sure, nonviolent means of defense and of liberation, ranging from peaceful forms of coercion—economic power, political agitation, mass demonstration, and the like—through passive resistance and noncooperation to rational and moral persuasion and even conversion of the enemy to a friend. To some degree these work in God's world. The message of the New Testament certainly speaks to Christians of a new and saving peace for the world that overcomes human warfare, and of a command not to defend oneself but to bear witness in a life that shares the servanthood and sacrifice of Christ. But here precisely lies the problem. Christ's victory is ultimate, both in undergirding the peace of human life today and in assurance that the final end of the world is in the hands of the triune God whom he revealed and not in those of human powers. But it is not penultimate. It cannot promise the preservation of this people's peace or the achievement of that people's justice here and now. The cross, as Reinhold Niebuhr so often said, is not a historical success story. Human fear and self-will have been conquered but they are still powerful. Those, therefore, who know themselves to be in the hands of the Redeemer will seek every way to transmute self-interest into public justice, dominating power into servant power, hatred and fear into fruitful relationships of trust, enemies into friends; but they will not imagine that this will suffice to prevent war in a sinful world. It is good politics, but it is not the whole of politics. The rest is still the balance of power against power to coerce that relative external peace and rough justice within which their internal and finer forms may flourish—and this despite the awful danger that the very act of violent power, or even too much preparation for it, may destroy what they are trying to defend.

But there is also a deeper, still more ambivalent reason why violence and war compel us. We are already caught, both materially and morally, in the conditions of which it is an element, and in the trends of which it is a consequence. Human beings are endowed by their Creator with inalienable dreams and ambitions. Life—including life in Christ under the promise of God—is self-affirming and filled with hope. We are called to abound, to cultivate the earth, and to organize human community for the peace and freedom of its members. Technology, science, economic enterprise, culture based on distinctions of language, custom, and ways of common life bring forth fruits that may glorify God and reflect his blessing. Yet this very human vitality, created and blessed and called by God, brings us into conflict with each other. Technology expands the possibilities for all human life and provides the tools whereby some societies exploit and dominate others. Economic expansion promises a higher standard of living for the whole world, and develops by a system in which the gap between rich and poor becomes ever greater. Structures of political power offer order and peace to some and oppression to others. Nor is there any refuge in moral principles, for the very ideals and standards of our society are a compound of respect for the divine judge of all peoples and the universalization of our own interests and culture into ultimate law.

We are all caught, therefore, in structures of justice and peace the relativity of which we recognize, which we want to reform and make better, but whose values we believe in and would defend. Others see those same structures as instruments of oppression and barriers to their justice and their peace. By our power, by our prosperity, and even more by our concept of what is right and good for the world, we are at war with them, even when bullets are not flying. Rightly or wrongly—and probably both—they attribute their pain and suffering to us. Rightly or wrongly, probably both, we regard them as threats to justice, freedom, and peace.

From this moral involvement with violence we can only very relatively withdraw, and even this withdrawal is an act within the involvement itself. It is possible, as some peace churches attempt, to bear witness to the judgment and promise of the kingdom of God by minimizing social participation in structures that do violence to others, not only the armed forces but exploitative industries and technologies as well, while maximizing opportunities for compromise of differences, and the building of relationships with would-be foes. But this requires a deliberate choice not to take responsibility beyond a certain point of moral ambiguity, for the balance of power in society and for the relative achievement of peace and justice there. It is, furthermore, always a judgment call, which balances responsible action in the world against witness to God's judgment on the world. Either way the moral involvement is there. The choice Christian pacifists make is, like all others in this sphere, only possible in repentance and the hope of forgiving grace.

This also puts the dilemma for the rest of us. We cannot retreat into romantic idealism, as if there were in human reason, in the spirit of love, in liberation from oppression, or in victory over totalitarianism, a solution to the problem of war. "We never have the chance," Niebuhr wrote more than forty years ago,

> to choose between tyranny and pure freedom; we can only choose between tyranny and relative democracy. We do not have the choice between war and perfect peace, but only between war and the uneasy peace of some fairly decent and stable equilibrium of social forces. We cannot choose between violence and non-violence, but only between violence and a statesmanship which seeks to adjust social forces without violence but cannot guarantee immunity from clashes. We have never had the opportunity—and probably never shall have—to choose between injustice and perfect equality, but only between injustice and a justice which moves toward equality and incorporates some of its values.[1]

We are responsible for defending the relative value of a social system that incorporates some of these possibilities, even as we try to reform it and feel the moral force of those outside to whom it is an instrument of violence. We are responsible for maintaining the tough balance of power which restrains the outbreak of greater violence, even while we fight the tendency to make that balance the overriding concern in the name of which peace and justice are themselves suppressed. There is no escape from this responsibility. If we evade it with easy illusions, if we refuse it on whatever grounds, we will answer for the consequences. There is also no escape from the moral ambivalence of violent, warlike action or intent. The people whose lives are destroyed are real and in them God judges our "just-war" criteria, our pretensions to be judges and executioners in our own cause. In the clash of these two principles lies the dilemma of Christian action in violence and war. War is compelling in its involvement of us all in its conflicts; it is inexorable in its overriding of all the moral limits and justifications we put upon it. Sherman was right. It is very much like hell.

Is there a way out of hell? Can we be delivered from the self-destructive compulsions of our interests and our ideals? Is there a reality that controls our destinies beyond the calculations of human power? If so, in what direction does it point us, and what hope does it give for the world in this age?

With questions like these the focus shifts. They are theological questions. Specifically for Christians they are about the divine-human reality within which the world has been placed by the life, death, and resurrection of Jesus Christ, and by the hope of his coming again. They concern, not the contrast between a transcendent ideal and a corrupt human condition, but the history of God's action in the midst of human powers and ambitions, fears and hopes, and the wars to which they lead. The first Christian inquiry then concerns this history. It involves discerning analysis of human warfare stripped of every illusion of justice or escape in the context of divine judgment and grace.

From this discernment, human action flows, not automatically but as a free response to the action of God. This is the context in which the ethics of war and peace belongs. The issue is not the moral rightness or the purity of the act itself, but the faithful witness of the believer to the redeeming presence of God in a world where no act is without sin and no policy without need of forgiveness for the wrong it does with its right. The aim is not goodness by a standard, but responsibility in a relationship with God and with the neighbor, not embodiment of the ultimate, but historical action for very relative goals offered to God for his use and correction. To explore the style of this response to God in the midst of human warfare is the second inquiry which concerns the Christian community.

It is the thesis of this essay that Christians in fact are driven to this way of reflection by the realities of human warfare and God's action in Jesus Christ. Such a thesis cannot be proved, but only illustrated. The examples which follow, two historical and one contemporary, attempt to do this. They are not exhaustive. They do not solve the problem of human conflict. But they do show the mind of the church at work at particular times, in the midst of, or before the menace of, war.

MARTIN LUTHER: CAN SOLDIERS BE SAVED?

Agony over the dilemma of participation in war is not new in Christendom. Not surprisingly it was posed with new force by the fact of the Reformation. Luther's teaching loosed a dynamic in human affairs that upset conventional controls and justifications in ways that even he was not always able to control. Better stated, he uncovered, with his doctrine of the free justification of the sinner by grace alone, profound struggles of conscience which had been carefully concealed in the medieval system of graded levels of perfection in the Christian life. This was the case especially in the practice of war. For centuries Catholic priests and monks (in contrast to the Orthodox) had not taken up arms. Their prayers and their dispensation of the church's grace had provided a refuge for souls endangered by the profession of soldiery. What now, when all Christians were called priests, and grace, with the life in Christ that flowed from it, was in full measure for everyone? Over the years a carefully elaborated moral structure had been developed to ease and guide the conscience of warriors on their level of secular existence in the initiation and conduct of war. What now, when this whole system of salvation by works, and the sacrament of penance that directed it, had been swept aside and the Christian found her- or himself commanded to participate directly with all her or his life and love, in community with the lord of grace? Some caught by this spirit drew its consequences without qualification: the Christian is a witness; she or he will not take up the sword; she or he will not participate in the coercive power of government in this world nor will she or he resist it save by the word that announces the judgment and redeeming love of Christ. It was not one of these, however, but a professional army man who put the question to Luther, "whether soldiers too (even soldiers!) can be saved?"[2]

Luther's answer was in one sense quite conventional, in another radically searching. On the one hand the kingdom of God and the kingdom of the world are sharply divided. God rules in the latter by force and violence if the situation demands it. Here an "external righteousness" is maintained by means of worldly government "which works through the sword so that those who do not want to be good and righteous to eternal life may be forced to become good and righteous in the eyes of the world. He administers this righteousness through the sword. And although God will not reward this kind of righteousness with eternal life, nonetheless he still wishes peace to be maintained among men and rewards them with temporal blessings."[3] So the military profession "is in itself a legitimate and godly calling and occupation." It is indeed the extension of the office of government to those situations in which it must defend itself from violence without, or violence within. As in the essay "On Temporal Authority" Luther brings to this argument, too, his strong preference for existing authority, even if tyrannous. To be sure, God is the judge in human affairs, and tyrants must expect that they will be punished for their cruelty and oppression, even by the uprising of the people or by external conquest. But the perspective of the soldier should be different. His job is to maintain order even if tyrannous, for no good comes of trying to overthrow a tyrant in the vain hope of getting a better ruler. Reason and experience combine to tell us that the violence done by warriors in the service of legitimate, even if unjust, authority prevents far more serious and general warfare. "The small lack of peace called war of the sword must set a limit to this universal, worldwide lack of peace which would destroy everyone."[4]

On the other hand none of this justifies either war, the soldier, or the ruler he serves.[5] At best it is an adjustment to the rough judgment of God in a world under the reign of sin and the devil, as incomprehensible in the light of Jesus Christ as some other events in nature and history which must be accepted as divine providence. The awfulness of war remains; such external justice as is granted it stands still under the judgment of God. Even wars of necessity, in lawful self-defense are, says Luther, human disasters. "Dear Lord," he would have the soldier pray, "you see that I have to go to war, though I would rather not. I do not trust, however, in the justice of my cause, but in your grace and mercy, for I know that if I were to rely in the justness of my cause and were confident because of it, you would rightly let me fall as one whose fall was just, because I relied on my being right and not upon your sheer grace and mercy."[6]

Nor is this a mere formula, apologizing to the Transcendent for doing what one knows by reason and experience is right and necessary anyway. Rather it places the Christian soldier in the middle of an active dialectic between the grace of God and the compelling evil of war. Only by turning away utterly from the desire to justify self, to assure his own salvation, only by throwing himself completely on the mercy of God, can a Christian—and how much more one whose profession is war and the preparation for war!— live and act in the midst of the necessities that compel him in this world. All works need forgiveness—above all, making war. When one finds oneself in the context of God's unmerited forgiving grace, however, then, within these necessities, discernment of those ways in which justice may become more sensitive to love becomes possible, and responsible action is informed by it. Luther is explicit and concrete on this. Having before condemned the peasants for the presumption and self-assertion in their rebellions, he condemns here the indiscriminate cruelty and the selfish motives by which the nobility suppressed them. Even external justice must be sensitive to degrees of guilt and the cry of human need. The defense of a country, he says, must be attempted with caution, with constant awareness of the way in which defense is mixed with greed and the lust for power. It is better to suffer loss than to let these baser motives get the upper hand. Peace, and not advantage, must be the goal. Furthermore there may come a time when the sovereign goes to war wrongly. Then the soldier should fear God rather than men and "neither fight nor serve, for you cannot have a good conscience before God."[7] He should refuse, not resist, and accept the loss and danger he incurs thereby, counting on the promises of the gospel. None of this is either self-justification or escape from the ambiguities of sinful choices. It is guidance for living responsibly in a world wherein faithful witness to the saving power of God requires accepting the guilt associated with right service of the neighbor.

Luther lived in the late medieval world. Although he undermined the status of government in theory, he attributed to it in practice far more service to justice than we can credit today. Although he set the Christian in the church free to live responsibly by grace, the scope he gave to free decision was limited. Nor was the reality of war as terrible, its unlimited dynamic as clear, as today. We need therefore another example of the method he embodies, closer to our time.

REINHOLD NIEBUHR: THE WAR THAT
MUST BE FOUGHT

Occasionally Niebuhr was capable of high dudgeon, as in his response to an editorial in *The Christian Century* on the eve of the American entrance into World War II. The *Century* had suggested that the difference between a just war and a holy war was so much "theological dust," and that those who must fight a war might as well give up on the idea of exercising moral restraint in doing so. Not so, said Niebuhr, "We can conceive of no more serious perversion of what the Christian faith means in its relation to all the proximate goals of justice in history than this interpretation." Holy war is a Muslim, or on a lower level a Nazi concept. "In terms of obvious historical facts it is folly to call such a cause as the defense of western democratic civilization 'holy'—in the sense that it is unqualifiedly good." The weapons we use are not holy; they are terrible. Our injustices which allowed such a terrible tyranny as Nazism to arise are those which we still must combat. Yet in all humility and repentance we must fight this war.

> The Christian worships a God whose goodness (holiness) transcends all forms of goodness known in history, all of which are tainted with sin. (Jesus was not throwing 'theological dust' into people's eyes when He declared: 'Why callest thou me good; no one is good save one that is God.') If we refuse to act because our cause or our weapons are tainted, we must either make inaction (contemplation) the final good of life, or we must assume that it might be possible to achieve a vantage point of pure holiness if only we could purge ourselves a little more. It is not possible to achieve this pure holiness; and yet we must act. The Christian acts with an uneasy conscience both because of the ambiguity of his cause and the impurity of his weapons. His conscience can be eased only as he is 'justified by faith,' and not by the achievement of holiness or by what is worse, the pretension of holiness.[8]

Justice is not holiness. Niebuhr meant something more by this than a distinction of grades in goodness. He was a child of Luther's Reformation. Sin is concern for self before the other, pretension to a greater goodness in one's cause, one's social system, or one's motives than they deserve. It is using one's very ideals to coerce others into submission to a good that is less than truly universal. It is an ingredient of all human structures and movements, attitudes and actions. We are justified by God's unmerited grace alone and in that freedom we seek such relative and imperfect justice in a sinful world as we can realize.

But Niebuhr went beyond Luther's division of two realms, into a thorough analysis of the "external righteousness" of this world. Justice for him is not defined by rational principles accessible to every mind. Nor is it the outworking of love applied by reason to a social situation. Rather, justice is discovered as it is constructed in the compromise of power with power and interest with interest, each submitting to a higher degree of mutuality. It presupposes an opposite reality to love: the self-affirmation of persons and groups. It demands coercive authority to protect it against breakdown into anarchy but must subject that authority to constant critique and opposition lest it become tyrannous. It is indeed "the highest rational moral ideal," because reason is capable of transmuting self-interest into more general principles of good. Yet "all rational justice constantly sinks to something less than justice"[9] because reason not only conceives the universal that judges the self; it also projects the universal in terms of the self. Justice breaks down when it is not continually challenged to higher degrees of mutuality by the spirit of love. Yet love is an ultimate reality that both fulfills and negates justice. It is complete giving of the self for the other which stands over and penetrates history in the cross of Christ. Only it, only God who so acts, is holy. Only he is good.

For Niebuhr to say therefore that a war is just does not mean what is expressed in standard just-war theory.[10] The Christian does not stand somewhere outside the struggle and make moral judgments on the whole. Rather one is in the midst of life with all its conflicts of power with power and with all the violence, real or potential, it involves. One is part of this power struggle, profiting from injustice while fighting for justice, aware of the relativity of one's cause, yet taking responsibility for it. In this situation, forgiven and inspired by God's grace and the love made known in Christ, one acts as responsibly as one can to improve the quality of justice in the world around one. As Niebuhr put it in the 1930s, humanity faces a double task: "The one is to reduce the anarchy of the world to some kind of immediately sufferable order and unity; and the other is to set these tentative and insecure unities and achievements under the criticism of the ultimate ideal."[11]

Working with this dialectical sense of the Christian life in public, Niebuhr has taken different attitudes toward different wars. He was a supporter of the First World War. Yet in keen awareness of the selfish misuse of power by the victors he called himself a pacifist, as a supporter of Woodrow Wilson's liberal internationalist peace aims:

> The very hope of the world and of civilization seems to lie in these aims. If the President succeeds in making them dominant and if the final peace conference will not content itself with territorial readjustments but will dedicate its energies to the abolition of international anarchy and the establishment of international order, civilization will be saved. If not, the war will have been lost no matter who wins it. This is the issue and the course for pacifists ought to be plain. Those who love peace must fashion the forces of war in the interest of their ideal and not content themselves with futile opposition to war itself.[12]

Throughout the 1920s Niebuhr's major theme was peacemaking in this sense. The struggle for justice must be transcended by the imperative of love. New covenants of peace—the League of Nations, the World Court—must be adhered to but the spirit of mutual trust and community must move beyond contractual agreements of just relations. "There can never be final peace until there will be nations who can in moments of crisis actually sacrifice their own rights for the good of the world." His image was that of the family of God subject to "the Christ Spirit of service and sacrifice."[13]

His well-dramatized change of emphasis in the 1930s brought out the other side of the dialectic but did not break its tension. The problem, he came to see, is violence within societies. Dominant powers coerce a certain order but as surely undermine it with the injustices they institutionalize. They rationalize their control with appeals to universal principles of justice, liberty, and peace which partly regulate them and partly are covers for their own interests. They grow even more harsh as their claim to righteousness goes unchallenged and their power unchecked. The first task then becomes not the transcendence of justice by love but the relative establishment of a rough justice by the (if necessary, violent) use of power by the victims of tyranny and exploitation. "The political task of dealing with the roots of social injustice must precede the moral task of building imaginative justice upon the foundations of the rough justice of politics."[14]

Thus Niebuhr described class warfare in the depths of the great Depression. But even then it was not his only word. There was never a time when he idealized that warfare or even described it as leading by itself beyond the rough justice of a balance of power. Those of the possessing classes he called to repentance, to the creation of structures relatively more just, and above all to recognition that revolutionary change must come as the just judgment of God. He organized Christians allied to or among the dispossessed to resist the self-righteousness of the executors of justice, to mitigate the violence that must come, and to prepare the way for continuing self-criticism and openness to reform within a socialist society. He would tolerate neither the liberal illusion that nonviolent methods can achieve all justice nor the Marxist illusion that the revolution itself brings justice and peace. We are compelled by our responsibility for our neighbor and by our present place in the conflict to participate in the power struggle for justice. We are caught in the unlimited character of that struggle, by the ideological tyranny of its leaders and the vindictive cruelty of its spirit. In this situation we live by grace which transmutes our righteousness and forgives our sins in the sacrificial love of God in Jesus Christ. By this grace and in this humility we seek to illumine and transform the justice of a violent world.

Against this background we can understand Niebuhr's outburst against *The Christian Century*. The struggle against Nazism was far less morally ambiguous than the class struggle. The temptation was therefore all the greater to make a human cause holy, or to exalt its justice into a self-justifying principle. But new corruption, new judgment, and new strife lie that way. "The Christian ought to know," he wrote in the depths of the Second World War,

> that we never have, in either individual or collective achievement, the perfect serenity of achieved ideals. Our peace is never a purely moral peace. Our final peace is the peace of forgiveness, of justification by faith. The Kingdom of God always remains fragmentary and corrupted in history. Even the highest historic achievement points beyond itself to a more final consummation even as every historic judgment points beyond itself to a more ultimate judgment. . . . Such 'other worldliness' is not an escape from history. It gives us a fulcrum from which we can operate in history. It gives us a faith by which we can seek to fulfill our historic tasks without illusion and without despair.[15]

The practical outcome of this theology was an unequivocal support of the war effort, a continual critique of American society in its conduct, and a constant emphasis on preparing to build the postwar peace. An awed sense of the terrible responsibility of the allied nations runs through the wartime pages of *Christianity and Crisis*, much of it expressed by Niebuhr himself. Warnings against self-righteousness, hatred, and an easy conscience mingle with forebodings that unless some tolerably just order can be built on the ruins of war with the participation of all, it may be fought in vain.[16] It seemed like a more sophisticated replay of the themes of twenty-five years before.

Not quite, however, for two reasons: the intransigence of the Soviet

Union, and the atomic bomb. The first of these was for Niebuhr a tyranny comparable, though less irrational and demonic, than the Nazi one that had just been conquered. The second was a tragic dilemma with which one could only live in perplexity and hope. In the post–World War II era, therefore, his dialectic expressed itself on three interlocking levels.

The first of these was a continuation of the social struggle of the interwar years. The terms, to be sure, had shifted. Soviet communism had shown the kind of new tyranny that self-righteous confidence in violent revolution brings. New Deal reforms in America, pragmatic socialist governments in Britain and India, and the rising determination of peoples in Western Europe and elsewhere to seek justice by balancing powers in a democratic system gave hope that the social power struggle need not be violent. Nevertheless Niebuhr recognized throughout this period that the terms of world social change may not be containable within democratic limits; the more so since the peoples of Asia and Africa are not only poor, but in rebellion against European and American dominance in the past. "The problem of America's 'moral' leadership," he wrote in 1946, "is thus the problem of whether our nation can rise above the modes of thought and behavior which are characteristic of a very wealthy nation, and understand the problems of nations as devoted as we to freedom but unable to afford the price we pay for it."[17]

Niebuhr put the matter more forcefully two years later:

> In our moral pride we think we are a beacon light of freedom to Asia. In our military pride we think we could win the battle against Communism in Asia by military might. The fact is that Asia is a continent in the throes of half a dozen revolutions at once. It is a colored continent, justly resenting the white man's arrogance. It is a continent of quasi-colonial peoples or of nations recently emancipated from colonial rule. The Asian peoples certainly do not understand the perils of Communism. But on the other hand they have no reason to believe that Democracy, as we understand it, would help them out of the morass of poverty.[18]

Niebuhr continually counselled (first toward China, then Africa, and finally Vietnam) the restraint of American political and military power in the Third World, and the effort to relate constructively to revolutionary forces and governments, even those with a Communist bent. The hope of cultivating an eventual democratic maturity underlay this counsel to be sure, but it would be a democracy whose justice would be defined not in America but in Asia and Africa themselves as responsible participants in an interdependent world.

This level of policy could not always be taken on its own terms, however, because of its continuous interaction with another, that of the power struggle between defenders of an open society in a democratic system on the one side, and the Communist ideal and practice on the other. The issue here was not capitalism versus socialism. It was not freedom versus justice or status quo versus revolution. It was not even peaceful versus violent change, for more than one nation found liberation through strife in those times. Rather, it was a struggle over the method by which these questions should be dealt with. In the early postwar years, before China produced an independent nonaligned Communist center, the line seemed to be drawn between an ideological system which allowed no place for self-criticism or dissent, backed by a military-political power with world ambitions on the one side, and all the nations and peoples who did not want to be so coerced on the other. What happened when this ideology and this power went unchecked was evident in Eastern Europe. It must be contained, forced into compromise, brought into relationships that will make impossible pursuit of its tyrannous ideal. Only thus can space be preserved within which the real struggle for justice and peace can take place.

Niebuhr has been labeled the theologian of the cold war. This is unfair. He was a theologian of containment and of new relations in the cold war. Containment was itself a compromise of justice for the sake of peace. It meant conceding a portion of the world to tyranny. It meant standing by when Soviet tanks crushed resistance in East Germany in 1953, in Hungary in 1956, in Czechoslovakia in 1968. The balance of power, he believed, was basic to any possible involvement, but not the use of power which might destroy that balance even for a just cause, or a better peace, with due prospect of success. Rather the way forward must be negotiation, the mitigation of tyranny by agreement which the power balance makes necessary and possible. It must be hoped that Soviet power and Communist ideology will soften and pluralize in a world that contains but does not threaten it.

To some degree this has happened. John Bennett has documented the ways in which Niebuhr perceived and responded to these changes.[19] But there was another dimension to his thought which placed the whole struggle under a more ultimate judgment. Containment and negotiation are responsible policies in a precarious world. They are not the formula by which we master our destiny. "The Irony of American History" is that Americans are unaware of the ambiguities of their own good causes and the temptations of their own power. So the very pursuit of a relatively just policy may fall to utter injustice because we claim a too-simple goodness for it, and do not take seriously the cries of those whom we harm. The relative responsible use of power may become thoroughly irresponsible because we do not recognize the limits of what foreign power can do, and the rejection it arouses. Unless power is held in repentance and humility, and unless that humility leads to restraint and sensitivity to the autonomy of the weak, at the proper time and place, it may be we who bring catastrophe to the world in the act of trying to save it. Vietnam was the last great example in Niebuhr's life. There have been several since.

This message is the witness of a church within a nation:

> The God before whom "the nations are as a drop in the bucket and are counted as small dust in the balances," is shown by faith and not by reason. The realm of mystery and meaning which encloses and finally makes sense out of the baffling configurations of history is not identical with any scheme of rational intelligibility. The faith which appropriates the meaning in mystery inevitably involves an experience of repentance for the false meanings which the pride of nations and cultures introduces into the pattern. Such repentance is the true source of charity; and we are more desperately in need of genuine charity than of more technocratic skills.[20]

WAR IN ITS NUCLEAR DIMENSIONS

Niebuhr died in 1971, twenty-six years into the era of nuclear weapons. He has been roundly criticized for the "Christian realism" of that period, most sharply of all for the third level on which he worked, his approach to the dilemma of nuclear armament.[21] There is no doubt that Niebuhr's originality did not shine in this area. He himself found no breakthrough, no way beyond the dilemma of holding a power in a precarious balance of mutual threat and terror, to use which would probably destroy the world. He lived within that dilemma, fighting off illusions about a survivable or winnable nuclear war on one side, and about the consequences of unilateral disarmament on the other. His hope lay, as it always had, in the coercion of competing powers into some tolerable and roughly just order, then in the subjection of that order to the leavening judgment of higher forms of mutuality which alone could save it from sliding once again into tyranny. "To walk the tightrope of our age, which is strung over the abyss of war and tyranny" is one description he gave of the Christian's task—in hope that on the far side the base will be firmer and the way wider. That such hope is reliable, he confidently believed. But "hope that is seen is not hope." He did not see the way forward.

Do we? The question at issue is not our evaluation of Niebuhr's political views in the last years of his life, but of his way of being Christian in the Reformation style, confronted with the challenges of war and peacemaking. What is involved in this way when we confront the dilemma of nuclear arms? I suggest four guidelines.

First, here, as in every political confrontation throughout history, the struggle for peace and justice begins with the search for some balance of power. No authority is good enough to rule without restraint. No ideology is rational enough to project an idea of justice and peace which truly includes the rights of the group whose interests produce it. Some form of power is essential to any group which would make its cry for justice respected and heard. A more universal justice beyond ideologies is always defined in the negotiation among social groups that can to some degree enforce their claims. The invention of nuclear weapons has not changed this. Despite Jonathan Schell's eloquent appeal,[22] human will to power has not been cowed by being raised to nuclear dimensions. Human self-justification has not been converted to universal reason by the awful logic of nuclear destruction.

In nuclear terms this means that the use of nuclear weapons by those who possess them is only effectively deterred by a counterforce capable of inflicting unacceptable damage on the attacker. This means that the much maligned policy of deterrence is—not the goal or the direction, or the sufficient answer—but the starting point and necessary condition of those international relations that might lead to peace. The policy of deterrence must not be celebrated as a means of security in itself, not turned into the central thrust of policy—but maintained as a fragile relative loom on which to weave the fabric of peace.

The problem with this approach is standard fare in moral discourse. Can one rightly threaten to do what it would never be permissible to do in fact: blow up the cities of a nation in a counterstrike? Can one hold the future of the world as a place of habitation hostage for the precarious freedom to work out one's own destiny that a balance of terror gives? There are no answers to these save counterquestions. Can one disarm unilaterally and leave the power of total destruction in the hands of an adversary alone? Would the renunciation of a credible deterrent in fact lead to peace or to more general, probably also nuclear, war? The blunt fact is that no policy in this area is "morally permissible." One must ask rather what policy gives some promise of that rough peace and order in the world on which higher levels of justice and community can be built. We must pursue that policy— depending not on our works, but on God's forgiving grace for our justification.

In fact this is what we do, despite our various protestations. George Kennan takes it as a premise in his proposals for a pledge of no first use, deep unilateral cuts in strategic arms, and denuclearization of Europe.[23] Alan Geyer attacks the "dogma" of deterrence with twenty-one criticisms through a whole chapter of his *The Idea of Disarmament*, only to admit at the end that a policy of deterrence has value as long as it is not turned into a total theory of security.[24] The American Roman Catholic Bishops' pastoral letter on war and peace, after setting forth traditional just-war criteria in its opening chapter, becomes thoroughly Lutheran-Niebuhrian in its treatment of the unavoidable necessity of a carefully circumscribed deterrence strategy. The report of the World Council of Churches public hearing on nuclear weapons adds a new complexity to the issue:

> The so-called "nuclear deterrent" is now a highly sophisticated and complex set of options, posing a wide variety of threats to an opponent, subject to constant change, and tending to encourage detailed planning about the way the options could be used in actual fighting.[25]

To maintain a credible deterrent, as a deterrent and no more, offering a maximum of inducement to the parties to negotiate more positive agreements, is itself a peacemaking art, constantly threatened by delusions of a fightable nuclear war on the one side and a rationally sinless human nature on the other.

Second, any balance of power, including nuclear deterrence, will break down into warfare unless it is continually leavened by the active pursuit of higher covenants of justice between or among the parties. The failure to seek this is the most terrifying dimension of the present policy of the United States under the Reagan administration. The balance of power among adversaries is not peace in any but the most meager sense of the word. It produces neither security nor justice; these depend on building relations of trust and mutual affirmation. They are the goal of the peacemaking process as surely as a balance of power is its premise. Realism about the adversary's power must be matched with growing perception of the adversary's interests in their overlap with one's own, and the adversary's needs and hopes as they interact with one's own. From this new and more sophisticated structures of mutually agreed order may arise: arms limitation or trade agreements, cultural exchanges, frank discussions of opposing ideologies, and more. Without it, deterrence itself will one day break down.

This is not a new insight among nonpacifist Christians. Niebuhr expressed it in his first published response to the atomic bomb, suggesting that to break down the fear and mistrust between the Soviet Union and the United States is a fundamental requirement of peace in an atomic age.[26] It was voiced in the theologians' report on *Atomic Warfare and the Christian Faith* in 1946 as a call for international control by civilian agencies of atomic research and production.[27] The so-called Dun Report to the Federal Council of Churches in 1950 on *The Christian Conscience and Weapons of Mass Destruction* devoted its concluding pages to a positive peace program including new relations with developing nations and reconciliation with the Soviet Union and its satellites.[28] Niebuhr again, in his last substantial contribution to the subject, analyzed signs of hope in the post-Stalinist Soviet Union that might open the way for peaceful diplomacy, trade, and cultural interpenetration.[29] In more recent years relations between churches in the Soviet Union and the United States have grown and deepened, even to the point of discussing problems of nuclear arms and disarmament in a Christian context.

The difficulty with all of this of course is that within these growing relations a tension develops. The claims of justice and of human rights raise their voices and tend to disrupt the growing friendship among the power-brokers. How much attention should Soviet diplomats or even private citizens pay to the poverty in our cities, to racial injustice, to the brutal inequities of our system? How much attention should we pay to persecuted Jews or Christian groups? to the suppression of dissident intellectuals? to the misuse of justice and denial of human rights in the Soviet Union? Yet there is a certain space for free play here. None of these relations threatens the power balance, unless they are blatantly used for propaganda warfare. Tactfully used, such probes of each other can build relations by showing how friendship is consistent with deep mutual questioning. They open the way for other, more subtle forms of power than the military to operate in more humane contexts than nuclear confrontation. Thus the fabric of peace is woven.

Third, negotiation and the development of agreements that limit arms and develop peace cannot be carried out without an element of creative risk. Absolute security is a false god that destroys its worshipers. This is partly an ideological problem. We come to identify our peace with the existence of friendly governments with certain social systems in crucial parts of the world. We read the East-West conflict into struggles that have quite other roots and motives. But it also is a matter of military and geopolitical calculations. Certain military advantages in certain weapons systems or certain theaters of potential war do have to be risked in any agreement on arms control. Certain possibilities for certain hostile industrial or technological developments are opened up in almost every trade agreement—even in the grain deals that feed Soviet technicians and factory workers. Recent debates over SALT II and other arms limitations proposals reveal how impossible it is to produce any risk-proof proposal which does not depend in some degree on an element of trust.

This trusting risk, based on shrewd and sensitive appreciation of the adversary's motives and interests as well as its powers and capacities, is good politics. Without it a nation is lost in a psychosis of fear and suspicion and cannot serve its own interests well. But it depends on a resource akin to love which a political body cannot easily give to itself. As Niebuhr said:

> The kind of humility which is required of nations to meet the possession of their new powers may be partly achieved by a shrewd political intelligence, which is able to measure the probable effect of certain policies upon the attitudes of other nations. . . . But ultimately this humility is a religious achievement. Rather it is not so much an achievement as a gift of grace, a by-product of the faith which discerns life in its total dimension and senses the divine judgment that stands above all human judgments.[30]

In this spirit the Presbyterian Confession of 1967 declares:

> The church, in its own life, is called to practice the forgiveness of enemies and to commend to the nations as practical politics the search for cooperation and peace. This search requires that nations pursue fresh and responsible relations across every line of conflict, even at risk to national security, to reduce areas of strife and to broaden international understanding.[31]

Finally, there may come a time in the politics of nuclear weaponry, as it has already come more than once in other international diplomacy, when a deliberate recognition of the limits of our power, and a deliberate renunciation of the effort to assert it, will be called for. It is hardly possible to foresee such a time. A study report of the World Council of Churches in 1958 suggested that it might come after a first strike had been launched against us, and no political purpose but vengeance could be served by launching a second strike.[32] It might arise after tactical nuclear weapons have been used by the enemy, in a deliberate decision not to save the battle by escalation. It could involve a decision not to move into space, or into the polar regions with nuclear arms, even though our adversary is doing it. It could be expressed right now in a no-first-strike commitment despite the disadvantages that would result on the European front.

It is not the particular case that is here at issue, however, but the fundamental readiness of holders of great power to recognize the limits of their responsibility for that power, and of their capacity to make it serve their ends. In Luther's terms there is a time when a soldier may not fight because he knows the war is wrong. As Niebuhr would put it, the relative righteousness of our cause can be turned in an instant to total unrighteousness if at the right time we do not recognize the judgment of God and surrender that cause into his hands. There is an ultimacy to this act that permeates the entire approach to war and its prevention. We human beings are not in control of the coercive power of which war is the fullest expression. We can neither escape our responsibility for our part in it, nor submit it to the control of our rational moral standards, nor manipulate it with a "realist" strategy toward desirable ends (as some humanist followers of Niebuhr have imagined). We are witnesses, not managers, stewards of relative gifts and responsibilities in our time and place, objects of forgiving and correcting grace for the wrong we do in our very struggle for justice and peace. We do not know with certainty the outcome of our efforts when we are powerful and strong; how much less when in some ultimate moment we must surrender that power and hope only in God. But we can hope in God in that moment also because hope has been the style of life to which we have been called all along. There is a future promise. We do not see it now, and it does not help to project ideals about it that are not rooted in responsibilities here before us. But in Christ we know its quality, and its signs give direction in the midst of human conflicts, even in nuclear war.

NOTES

1. Reinhold Niebuhr, *Christianity and Power Politics* (New York: Charles Scribner's Sons, 1940), 75–76.

2. The German title of this essay, "Ob Kriegesleute auch in seligem Stande sein können," is less sharply put than the English, but the English brings out a point. For Luther it is God's justifying *act* in the midst of human acts that counts.

3. "Whether Soldiers, Too, Can Be Saved," in *Luther's Works* (Philadelphia: Fortress Press, 1967), 46:99–100.

4. Ibid., 96.

5. Per contra, Paul Ramsey: "[Luther] states that moral decisions coming from a free mind are 'given by love and by the law of nature of which the reason is full'" (*The Just War* [New York: Charles Scribner's Sons, 1968], xiii). But this quotation from "On Temporal Authority" is taken out of the context of Luther's sharp dialectical understanding of both reason and justice.

6. "Whether Soldiers, Too, Can Be Saved," 123.

7. Ibid., 130.

8. *Christianity and Crisis*, vol. 1, no. 19 (November 3, 1941): 1.

9. Harry R. Davis and Robert C. Good, eds., *Reinhold Niebuhr on Politics* (New York: Charles Scribner's Sons, 1960), 164.

10. In expounding the just-war principle of proportionality, Ramsey writes:

"All that Reinhold Niebuhr ever said about politics and war falls under this heading, since the principle of proportion says simply that nations, statesmen and citizens are acting responsibly when they choose and vigorously support policies and decisions which are likely to secure the lesser evil (or the greater good) among their mixed consequences" (*The Just War*, 429).

If Niebuhr thought that nations, statesmen, and citizens were dispassionate, objective, rational agents, this would be true. In fact, for Niebuhr the perception of injustice involves the whole person in encounter with both God and the neighbor, learning truth by repentance for the way pride distorts moral reason along with every other expression of the self.

11. Reinhold Niebuhr, *An Interpretation of Christian Ethics* (Minneapolis: Winston Press, 1979), 38.

12. William G. Chrystal, ed., *Young Reinhold Niebuhr: His Early Writings, 1911–1931* (St. Louis: Eden Publishing, 1977), 100. The words were written in 1919.

13. Ibid., 208. From a 1928 speech.

14. Reinhold Niebuhr, *Reflections on the End of an Era* (New York and London: Charles Scribner's Sons, 1934), 234–35.

15. *Christianity and Society* 9 (Winter 1943): 12.

16. On the responsible conduct of the war, e.g., "Our Responsibilities in 1942," vol. 1, no. 24 (January 12, 1942); "The Evacuation of Japanese Citizens," vol. 2, no. 8 (May 18, 1942); "The Just War of Unjust Nations," vol. 3, no. 1 (February 8, 1943); "Is the Bombing Necessary?" vol. 4, no. 5 (April 3, 1944).

On postwar responsibility, e.g., "America and the Peace After the War," vol. 1, no. 4 (March 24, 1941); "Plans for World Reorganization," vol. 2, no. 17 (October 9, 1942); "Anglo-Saxon Destiny and Responsibility," vol. 3, no. 16 (October 4, 1943); "Soberness in Victory," vol. 5, no. 9 (May 28, 1945).

17. "As Others See Us," *Christianity and Crisis*, vol. 6, no. 21 (December 9, 1946).

18. *Christianity and Society* 13 (Spring 1948).

19. "Neibuhr's Ethic: The Later Years," *Christianity and Crisis* 42 (April 12, 1982).

20. Reinhold Niebuhr, *The Irony of American History* (New York: Charles Scribner's Sons, 1952), 150.

21. So Alan Geyer: "He not only discounted pacifists: he scorned disarmament, the UN, collective security, world community, international law, and peace research" (*The Idea of Disarmament: Rethinking the Unthinkable* [Elgin, Ill.: Brethren Press, 1982], 200). The wrongness of this judgment is so monumental as to raise the question through what distorting prism so competent a modern scholar was looking, to obscure the fundamentals of Niebuhr's perspective and raise his occasional thoughts to absolutes. For the record, Niebuhr attacked utopian illusions about disarmament, the UN, collective security, world community, international law, and peace research because he was so deeply committed to the reality of them all. To face the facts of the modern power conflict in all their starkness is not to be a cold warrior. To surrender illusions is not to lose, but to lay the foundation of, a confident hope.

22. Jonathan Schell, *The Fate of the Earth* (New York: Alfred A. Knopf, 1982). Originally appearing in the *New Yorker*, this book dramatized the nuclear threat, and aroused considerable public concern.

23. George Kennan, *The Nuclear Delusion: Soviet-American Relations in the Atomic Age* (New York: Pantheon Books, 1982), 186–87.

24. Geyer, *The Idea of Disarmament*, chap. 2, pp. 58–59.

25. Paul Albrecht and Ninan Koshy, eds., *Before It's Too Late* (Geneva: World Council of Churches, 1983), 8.

26. *Christianity and Crisis*, vol. 5, no. 17 (October 15, 1945).

27. *Atomic Warfare and the Christian Faith*, Report of the Commission on the Relation of the Church to the War in the Light of the Christian Faith (New York: Federal Council of Churches, 1946), 15ff. The sharpest point in this report was the judgment that "the surprise bombing of Hiroshima and Nagasaki are morally indefensible" (p. 11).

28. *The Christian Conscience and Weapons of Mass Destruction*, Report of a Special Commission appointed by the Federal Council of Churches (New York, 1950), 20ff.

29. Reinhold Niebuhr, *The Structure of Nations and Empires* (New York: Charles Scribner's Sons, 1959), 281ff.

30. Reinhold Niebuhr, *Discerning the Signs of the Times: Sermons for Today and Tomorrow* (New York: Charles Scribner's Sons; London: SCM Press, 1946), 66–77.

31. "The Confession of 1967," Part II, section A, 4, b, in *The Book of Confessions* (New York: Presbyterian Church in the United States).

32. *Christians and the Prevention of War in an Atomic Age*, a study document of the World Council of Churches (1958), chap. V.

5

NEITHER GUERRILLA
NOR *CONQUISTA:* THE PRESENCE OF
THE KINGDOM AS SOCIAL ETHIC

JOHN H. YODER

My assigned topic was first identified as "The Peace Church Ecclesiological Ethical Model." Later it was formulated "The Ethics of the Minority."
The first phrasing was jargon. We shall find the second, the reference to
minority status, to be illuminating, but it mistakenly leads us toward thinking that the matter is primarily quantitative. We could speak of "the temptation of establishment," yet that puts the question too juridically, and we
live in a country where the mention of "establishment" is rendered confus-
ing by the federal government's being forbidden to deal with one form of it
(establishment of religion). We could speak in habitual sociological terms
of the ethics of the "sect," but as I shall show that would prejudge the
question. Rather than seeking to discover or to coin some new untainted
term, I propose to continue to use all of the above, each where it is most
illuminating, but recognizing that none alone is fully satisfactory.

One might approach the topic by repeating earlier helpful analyses. The
years have confirmed the aptness of observing that a distinctive stance in
social ethics both follows from and contributes to a distinctive social loca-
tion. There are still corners of the ethical field where that awareness had
not penetrated. In its essence, however, the point was already established
by Ernst Troeltsch, and will not be repeated here.

It would not be out of place in this context to unfold, with the help of
examples, the reasonableness of the connection between the social status in
which radical Reformation communities have usually found themselves in

---

John H. Yoder is professor of theology at the University of Notre Dame, and has also taught
in the Associated Mennonite Seminaries in Elkhart, Indiana. He is author of numerous
works including *The Politics of Jesus* (Grand Rapids: Wm. B. Eerdmans, 1972), and *The
Priestly Kingdom* (Notre Dame, Ind.: University of Notre Dame Press, 1985), in which this
chapter also appears, in slightly modified form.

the post-Renaissance West and the specific social style which they have developed: migration, pacifism, vocational specialization. But this too has been done repeatedly and, some might think, repetitively.

It is also possible to trivialize our topic with ecumenical good manners. In an age when every confessional family is willing to recognize that others have something to say, it is natural that some of the churches of the majority Western traditions should take notice of the distinctive "peace church" presence as one of those families whose witness had not been heard, and to which it would be appropriate to give attention. Since it is assumed that every denominational family must possess some charisma that the others should hear of, and since the phrase "peace church" has become accepted,[1] the suggestion normally arises that on the questions of war and peace the peace churches could be helpful to other groups whose traditions are less focused in this regard.

Intentions to learn from the peace churches have been expressed by both the World Council of Churches and the Lutheran World Federation. Quite recently the suggestion has even been voiced that other denominations might declare themselves to be peace churches by adopting some kind of antimilitary statement.

We see here at work the ordinary ethos of liberal Western ecumenism. One assumes that it is proper for each denominational communion to have their "thing," perhaps thought of as their "gift" in analogy to the language of 1 Corinthians 12, or as their "talent." One assumes that each denomination's particularity is somehow "true," in that others should listen to it respectfully, rather than calling it heretical as they used to do. At the same time, one assumes that the kind of "truths" which the others hold is not overpowering, since that "respectful listening" does not obligate one to agree with them, or even to weigh seriously the reasons *they* give for their views. One listens to the others when and because one has one's own timely reasons to think that what they say might be interesting; one listens to them on one's own terms and at one's own convenience. Thus the price of this good-mannered ecumenical openness to hear one another at our points of distinctiveness is a pluralism that may replace the truth question with a kind of uncritical celebration of diversity. Our recognition of how it is that those other people, from their other place in history, can hold to those other views does not necessarily mean expecting those views to have any hold on us because they can claim to be true or biblical or prophetic. After all, the ecumenical etiquette must be reciprocal. If I grant that what makes you distinctive is worth listening to, it is appropriate that you should return the compliment, and accept that my having been led in another direction is equally authentic.

A most dramatic form of such relativization by means of polite recognition was the development in Germany in 1958-59 of the notion of "complementarity" whereby "peace service with weapons" and "peace service without weapons" were declared to be reciprocally compatible, largely cutting the edge of the peace movement in German Protestantism for most of the next decade.

My assignment is to exposit, noncoercively and dialogically, the case for claiming that the stance which has here been variously labeled as "peace church," "minority," "nonestablished," "radical reformation" is closer to the gospel and more properly to be recognized as the imperative under which Christians stand than are the alternatives.

Instead of asking what ethical positions come naturally to a church that finds itself in a minority, or which ethical positions, if taken consistently, would probably leave any church in minority status, my task is to state that particular set of convictions about what should be the stance of the whole Christian community. This stance appears with peculiar force within the social context in which the community is outvoted, but its truth claims are not dependent on that social situation. I should not ask what complementary corrective is needed from a minority perspective after granting that the majority establishment does most of the work of being the church. I should ask rather what the whole church is called to be in the real world where it is (really) in a minority position. I shall use the memory and perspective of minority experience only to clarify the credibility of such positions, and to spark creativity about the possibility of a counterestablishment stance for the whole church—all this without granting either that Christians, if they took these positions, would always be voted down or excluded, or that it only makes sense to hold such positions when the believing community is numerically insignificant.

THE DIFFERENCE STATUS MAKES

It is not immediately obvious to all modern readers why it is important to take into account the minority status of a faith community in understanding its ethical perspectives. The perspective of the book of the Apocalypse, or of the prophecies of Jeremiah and Ezekiel, or for that matter of the records of the message of Jesus, cannot be grasped without recognition of that fact that these writers do not assume that their listeners or readers dominate the society where they live. Contemporary readers of such literature know that to be the case, yet many do not take account of that fact to explain why the ethical orientation projected in such literature takes the shape it does.

The way we put this question in modern times is itself the product of our times. It is only possible to think seriously about what difference it makes that a moral community is a minority, if one has come to grips with the difference that dominant status may make. Thus an indispensable detour toward our theme must be a sketchy inventory of the difference it makes, specifically for Christians, when the ethical guidance that they derive from their faith is adjusted to their having become the dominant element of their society.[2]

The ethical orientation may need to change in the minds of most when the ruler has become a member of the church. During the Christian Middle Ages Constantine became the symbol of this.[3] The assumption tends to be that in order to continue being a sovereign, a ruler needs to continue to act the way a (non-Christian) sovereign "naturally" acts, thereby creating some tension with what the later prophets and Jesus taught about domination, wealth, and violence. A strongly conversionist ethic might hold forth the possibility that a converted ruler could also transform the office and might resolve differently the challenges of dominion, wealth, and killing (much later there will be some conversionists with visions like that); but in the fourth century there was no recorded strong advocacy of the possibility that the conversion of Constantine might change his behavior or that of his heirs. We discover there what later Protestant social ethics will call the ethic of vocation, whereby the proper thing to do in one's given social setting is determined by the inherent, quasi-autonomous law of that setting,[4] the demands of which can be both known and fulfilled independently of any particular relation to the rootage of Christian faith.

The influx into the membership of the Christian church of larger numbers of persons, for whom that new affiliation is not the expression of a strong personal faith experience or commitment, means that there will be a need to adjust the expectations of ethical teachers with regard to how insightful and how unselfish we can ask people to be. The conversionist ethic of a minority under pressure can expect of its members a "heroic" level of devotion. A church of the multitudes, on the other hand, must be satisfied with a run-of-the-mill level of understanding and devotion. Here we discern the point of entry of two notions that the earlier Christians or the Jews of the same epoch would not have taken for granted:
- the notion of a distinction between the minimal morality of the "precepts" and the higher "volunteer" level of the "evangelical counsels," and
- the independent but congenial notion that the kind of life compatible with the call of the gospel is only manageable by virtue of some degree

of special motivation, usually expressed in a vocational withdrawal from ordinary life.

Once we dominate society, the way we want things to go is the way they might very well be able to go. One therefore can think of social behavior in terms of controlling social process or of goal-oriented causation. The rightness or wrongness of behavior can now be translated or interpreted in terms of good and bad outcomes. If we want something not to happen we can declare it a crime, we can punish it when it does happen, and it will happen less frequently or not at all. If we want something to happen, we can make it an obligation or reward it, and it will tend to happen. Thus there enters into ethical thought

- that entire set of styles of discourse which later analysis will speak of as teleological or utilitarian, that is, as orienting evaluation around intended or actually achieved outcomes, as well as
- the distinguishable but compatible notions of "compromise" and the "lesser evil," whereby it is a part of moral decision to play against one another a variety of competitive values that are at stake, and to take responsibility for the particular value-mix and cost/benefit trade-off that will come out to be the most desirable "for the good of the whole."

Behind these adjustments, where the logic flows from the changed social setting to a changed pattern of ethics, it will then be natural to develop as well a changed set of expressed philosophical or semantic assumptions. It will now be appropriate to speak about nature and grace in such a way as to affirm the knowability through "nature" of kinds of moral insight that correspond to the new ethic. It will be assumed that the moral insights of gentile antiquity and the teachings of the Old Testament are for some reason closer to "nature" than are the teachings and example of Jesus. The general tone of the argument will be formal: that is, it will seek to show why one should believe in general that those other sources of moral guidance may have some validity. Yet the stake in the argument is material. Those other moralities are more affirmative than is the New Testament about the uses of coercion, violence, wealth, status, tradition, and the justification of means by ends. Later versions of the same kind of reasoning for modern times will take account of non-Christian contemporaries and of other cultures, or of post-Christian skeptics in the West, as representative of the access that people may have moral insight apart from the channels of the community of faith.

It is not my present concern to project an argument about whether these changed approaches are biblically or logically or realistically acceptable, but only to report it as a matter of the history of Western moral thought that their coming to dominance in Christian and post-Christian thought is correlated with Christianity's becoming the faith of the dominant segment of society. They would not be thinkable in this same simplicity from the perspective of a persecuted or isolated minority. The way this evolution has been described retraces the path of the dominant thought of Christendom. As already noted, the ethicist will recognize it as touching the main traits of the form of social thought which Troeltsch called "churchly."

By charting the natural changes in social thought that derive logically and historically from the churches' acceptance of a position of social dominance, we have traced backhandedly the major traits that we shall expect obviously to characterize a church which (whether naively or self-consciously) seeks to live and to keep thinking in a setting parallel to that of the early Christians. But before we advance to the affirmative statement of what we have already projected obversely, let it be recalled that (contrary to the pattern of interpretation which generally dominates the reading of this story in the West) the initial intention of the "sectarian" communities, which in the course of Western history have renewed a minority ethic, has not been to be sects. Division has not been their intention. They have called upon all Christians to return to the ethic to which they themselves were called. They did not agree that their position was only for heroes, or that it was only possible for those who withdraw from the wider society. They did not agree to separate themselves from the church at large as more righteous. They rather called upon the church at large to accept as binding for all Christians the quality of commitment that would in effect lead them all to be separated from the world once again in order to be appropriately in mission to the world.

THE NOTION OF RADICAL
HISTORICAL CRITIQUE

What it takes to explain one group of people to another group will depend upon who the others are. There is no such thing as just one central definitional trait which characterizes the radical Reformation view, except as we specify what is the respective other position from which a given "radical" group differs. Let us begin our characterization of the radical Protestant Reformation with the very notion of challenging establishment: that is, of rejecting, or at least doubting fundamentally, the appropriateness of letting the Christian faith be the official ideology of a society, especially of the elite within a society.

Why then should there be anything wrong with Christianity's becoming an official ideology? It must be because that change itself calls into question something definitional about the faith. Perhaps this would not need absolutely to be the case.

It nonetheless tends to be the case, in the experience of the Christian community, that the only way in which the faith can become the official ideology of a power elite in a given society is if Jesus Christ ceases to be, concretely, Lord. Some other value: power, mammon, fame, efficacy, tends to become (the radical would say *must become*) the new functional equivalent of deity. The condemnation is then not addressed to popularity or visibility or social responsibility, not to growth in numbers or to toleration as such, but to purchasing such value at the expense of fidelity to Christ as Lord. It makes no difference for the present analysis whether the claims of some other lord than Jesus be made effective because a believer follows them out of the conviction that he or she should be serving an unbelieving community or whether the rejection of Jesus be more tacit or even unwitting. Nor does it matter whether we think of specific casuistic "crunch" decisions where someone chooses to do evil with a good intent or whether deeper matters of character and commitment be thought of as more basic.

Obviously it will never happen, at least not in the first generation, that anyone will say explicitly that another deity has been elevated beside Jesus Christ. They will rather say that these other values, which they call by less judgmental names like responsibility, nature, efficiency, wisdom, are also affirmed as a part of the meaning of "Christ," standing in some complementary relationship to the Lordship that is still ascribed to Jesus. This supplementary or complementary insight deals with some realm to which Jesus had not spoken, or fills in a gap which the radicality of the gospel had not taken time to treat. It takes its cues from other positive values which Jesus can hardly be against, like reason and created nature, like the orders which it takes to keep a society operating, even though at certain crunch points this means specifically not doing what Jesus said or did or asked of his disciples.[5] This peaceable complementarity seems self-evidently acceptable as a way to widen the relevance of the faith to more people and more questions. Only the distance of several generations later or unbelieving criticism will name the contradiction more bluntly.

If it is the case that this kind of adjustment to other loyalties is a step on the way to unfaithfulness and should be condemned, then it would seem at first that the necessary corrective would be to reject all change, restoring things as they had been before. For the early centuries the concept of "renewal" was this simple; it asked for the restitution of the way things had already been. Only in recent centuries has historical consciousness made it impossible to think that way. Any effort to restore what one thinks had been there before changes that ideal by the very fact that it is now being sought as the goal of retroactive change, whether or not one is successful in restoring it. For over a thousand years this was how both sides argued. The party of accommodation identified the changes they had made as movement forward, and accordingly the critics could conceive of no alternative but artificial movement backward.

The genuine alternatives arise when one faces the fact that neither of those pure options is real. No one can simply say that the movement up to the present has all been forward. The movement up to the present has not been all in one direction and has not brought us all to one place. One who criticizes the way things have come is not now proposing that they should somehow reverse history or "return to go," but that the way they have come should be recognized not to have been good, or not only good, and that a midcourse correction should be made in the light of a better picture of where they should have gone. The reference of the "radicals" to the early centuries is then not made with a view to undoing the passage of time but with a view to properly reorienting our movement forward from the present in light of what we now know was wrong with the way we had been going before.[6]

The truth claims being made by the critics of the unfaithfulness into which Christians have fallen through the centuries are therefore not posited upon a vision of some pristine clarity that could be rejoined by going back to the first century. That is a frequent misconception of what the Protestant Reformation in general and the radical Reformation in particular were about. The point is rather that they deny such absolute authority to any other epoch, especially to the present, and especially to arrangements that came about in the medieval period through a tacit or explicit relativizing of the normative power of the incarnation. It is those who believe their own present truths to be the culmination of univocal progress who are unaware of historical relativity and whose truth claims are circular (and almost always elitist). The critic whose historical criticism is rooted in the Bible admits the risks of particularity by that way of putting the question.

This appeal to Scripture as judge over our unfaithfulness came into the classical documents of Protestants out of the dramatic situation of historic schism. That context should not be permitted to make us think that schism is its normal form. Its normal form is rather the regular exercise of the office of teacher in the Christian community. It is regularly, and in regular circumstances, the function of the *didaskalos* ("teacher") to serve peaceably as the instrument of tense interaction between the community's memory and its contemporary articulation. We must express our faith in terms that make sense to our neighbors in their own language, we must face the challenges with which they live, and at the same time defend against selling out, against cheap conformity, by finding new and relevant ways to remind ourselves that it is always the God of Abraham and the Father of Jesus about whom we are talking. Ordinarily, when the gift of *didaskalos* is being properly exercised and the contribution of the bearer of that gift is being properly received, this procedure of reminding and remembering operates in a permanent reciprocity of exchange between the concern for contemporary relevance and the concern for historic community unity.

The appeal to canonical origin provokes division only when some other power in the community has subtracted itself from the purview of the appeal to Jesus, or when the *didaskalos* has fallen into inflexible modes of articulation. The act of looking back to the origins, which in cases of radical Reformation provokes the crystallization of new and independent forms, should normally not take that dramatic shape. The proper exercise of the moderating vocation of *episkopos* ("overseer") will normally find ways to let the renewing reminder of our rootage in Jesus be effective without division.[7]

It is thus not a part of the definition of the "radical Reformation" position that it should go beyond some other reformation. What is definitional is the ultimate normative claim of the appeal to Jesus. In extreme circumstances, in the face of entrenched apostasy, it is true that the readiness to take the shape of a radical Reformation—that is, the readiness to let the price of faithfulness be expulsion from the established mainstream—may be the test of faithfulness. Yet what matters to the radical Reformation position is not its radicality but its Lord. In situations where that appeal to the normativeness of Jesus does not trigger defensive expulsions, the free church has no commitment to schism or to extremism.

MINORITY LANGUAGE, MAINSTREAM VOICES

I must therefore not describe the orientation that I advocate as an updating of something modeled by Peter Cheltchitzki or by Pilgram Marpeck or by George Fox. Those "radical" positions were worked out by people who had been expelled from the regnant Christian community without a serious hearing. They therefore represented responses to exile as much as they did projections of the shape of the faithful community. I am more interested in finding *within* majority Christianity people who at least begin to ask the right questions, even though their being in the majority position may keep them from following those questions to their natural conclusions.

Two generations of college students have come to know the heritage of H. Richard Niebuhr, mostly through his *Christ and Culture*, originally published in 1951. The book is a most impressive synthetic vision of how the variety of different positions that Christians take all make sense, each in its own place, and how they all need each other, culminating in the best case being made for the most complex and pluralistic of the five typical orientations. Some whose picture of H. Richard Niebuhr is the product of that book would be surprised to encounter his 1935 work, *The Church Against the World*.

> The world has always been against the church, but there have been times when the world has been partially converted and when the churches lived with it in some measure of peace; there have been other times when the world was openly hostile, seeking to convert the church. We live, it is evident, in a time of hostility, when the church is imperiled not only by an external worldliness but by one that has established itself within the Christian camp. Our position is inside a church which has been on the retreat and which has made compromises with the enemy in thought, in organization, and in discipline. . . .
>
> Only a new withdrawal followed by a new aggression can save the church and restore to it the salt with which to savor society.[8]

H. Richard Niebuhr spoke of the church as being in bondage to idolatry, to capitalism and nationalism and the spirit of class, but also to optimistic humanism, to a too-easy identification of the church with worthwhile social causes and valuable human experiences. Companion essays by Wilhelm Pauck and Francis Miller elaborated further the critique of the liberal identification of the church with worthy causes and human self-fulfillment.

This call to the church to rediscover an identity of its own did not mean a call back to some earlier phase of Protestant integrity. These writers were neither "evangelical" nor "neo-orthodox." Niebuhr, Pauck, and Miller wrote from within the mainstream of cooperative and intellectually and socially liberal Protestants. It is perhaps partly for that reason that their witness has been forgotten. It is nonetheless historically noteworthy that from the academic and ecclesiastical perspectives from which these men wrote—Niebuhr had been president of a denominational college, and, when the above essay was published, was teaching ethics at a divinity school; Pauck was an immigrant Reformation historian interpreting the contemporary crisis in European Protestantism in order to throw light on the American experience; Miller had twenty years' experience in the World Student Christian Movement—together they could say that the church must begin by affirming an identity not derived from, or tailored for, a contribution to society, but from a stance independent of the established institutions.

A decade later, John C. Bennett, in *Christian Ethics and Social Policy*, provided a pluralistic synthesis somewhat like *Christ and Culture*. He described five different social strategies, among which the fifth is the most adequate, the most flexible, and the least clearly defined. Yet somewhat independently of that discussion of ethical orientations toward society as a whole, Bennett also restated a distinctive vision for the church as a community. The church, he said, should be

a base for operation in a world that is still alien . . . an ethical laboratory . . . to push further in the realization of Christian goals for human life than can be done in society at large . . . a school to train for dual citizenship . . . and a voice of criticism that continues to sound when most other voices have been silenced.[9]

H. Richard Niebuhr did not write his next book about the church against the world. One can even argue that his pluralistic typology later in *Christ and Culture* was his apology for backing away from so decisive a judgmental stance, or for not having found a church to fit that vision. Similarly, the later published work of Bennett was not devoted to working out more fully his vision of the church as community over against the world. It cannot be said that he retreated from that affirmation; but most of the time it was not his calling to be sharpening it.[10]

The following summary can best be understood as an effort to formulate what Bennett and H. Richard Niebuhr would have said if they had gone on with the direction suggested in the texts here cited. Niebuhr, Pauck, and Miller say on the grounds of theological integrity that if the church testifies to a God who is other than or more than our best common sense, then it must stand over against the world and the world's wisdom. Bennett says that if the things the church wants to help Christians do in the wider society, and help the wider society do for itself, are to have direction and integrity, there must be an empirical body of people who help one another define and fulfill the concrete social meaning of their loyalty to Jesus Christ. That logic is intrinsically authentic, whether or not to the people testifying to it who have been pushed thereby into ecclesiastical separation.

We know that it is congruent with the radical ecclesiology to be nonviolent in a violent world, and not to take signals from the consensus of the world. What more can be said of its style?

THE WEIGHT OF WEAKNESS

The believing community as an empirical social entity is a power for change. To band together in common dissidence provides a kind of social leverage that is not provided by any other social form. The subordinate community with its own internal covenants is able to provide support to individuals who could not stand alone against the stream.

- There is the psychic or moral support of knowing that others see it my way.
- There is the psychic support of others who are up when I am down, to prevent the activist from feeling indispensable.
- There is the far more concrete support of social security and survivor's aid. The early Hutterian and Quaker missionaries were courageous in risking their lives abroad because they knew that if they did not return their loved ones would be taken care of.[11]
- There is a special form of psychic support which helps us live up to our stated goals. If I have secretly told myself, in the face of some challenge, that I will go thus far and no farther, and then the challenge goes a little farther, I may, if I am standing alone, give in a little more. If, however, I have covenanted with you to go no farther than that, our solidarity will augment my power to resist. This is the psychic power of Alcoholics Anonymous; why should it not also guard against other intoxications?
- There is refuge in a wider supporting community for people who, because of their dissent, are driven from home or livelihood or land.
- There is mutual support for dissenters in that their combined power of resistance is far more than the sum of the resistance potential of each member taken separately. When one leader is "burned out" the others are rested. When one is shot down another can step into her or his place. No one of them needs to carry the whole burden of responsibility alone. What modern analysis calls the division of labor and the New Testament calls the diversity of gifts makes the organism as a whole more efficient than if each individual were endeavoring to stand against the stream alone. Thus the plurality of members of the body provides not simply more strength quantitatively but more skills and special contributions qualitatively.
- There is hope for the future. When the powers of evil are for a time so successful that all resistance seems to be crushed, it is from the ranks of that community, just now bludgeoned into quiescence, that another generation's prophets, in their time, will come.

FIRST FRUITS

The alternative community discharges a modeling mission. The church is called now to be what the world is called ultimately to be. Jews and Christians classically described their community in terms like those employed by the wider world: people, nation, kingdom, even army. This is not simply a poetic figure of speech. It means the claim to see oneself, and to need to be worthy to be seen, as doing for and on behalf of the wider world what the world is destined for in God's creative purpose. The church then is not a chaplain or priest to the powers running the world: it is called to be a microcosm of the wider society not only as an idea but also in its functioning.

1. The church undertakes pilot programs to meet previously unmet needs or to restore ministries that have collapsed. The church is more able to experiment because not all ministries need to pay off. One can take the risk of losing or failing, more than can people in charge of the state. The examples generally referred to in this realm are the way in which popular education, institutionalized medicine, and the very concept of dialogical democracy in the Anglo-Saxon world generalize patterns that were first of all experimented with and made sense of in Free-church Christianity.

2. The church represents a pedestal or a subculture in which some truths are more evidently meaningful and some lines of logic can be more clearly spelled out than in society as a whole. The credibility and the comprehensibility of an alternative vision which an original prophetic person can claim is enormously more credible and comprehensible if it is tested, confirmed, and practiced by community. This theme will return under another heading later as well.

3. In more classical Christian terms, there is the notion of "sacramentality," which means that sets of meanings that make sense on an ordinary level make more of the same kind of sense when they are embedded in the particular history of the witness of faith. Catholics now talk about the existence of the church as itself a "sacrament," in the sense that the church represents the kind of society that all of society ought to be. The church is able to be that because of the presence in its midst of witness and empowerment which are not in the same way accessible to the wider society. Sometimes this sacramental quality calls us to say about the church what we say about the rest of society. For instance, if in society we believe in the rights of employees then the church should be the first employer to deal with workers fairly. If in the wider society we call for the overcoming of racism or sexism or materialism, then the church should be the place where that possibility first becomes real.

More striking and more concrete cases of "sacramentality" can be developed if we look at those specific activities which the church has more traditionally called "sacraments." Here the logic flows the other way—from what the sacrament means to what the world should be.

- The Eucharist originally was, and could again become, an expression not only of the death of Christ for our sins but also of the sharing of bread between those who have and those who have not.

- Baptism could again come to be, as it was in the New Testament, the basis of Christian egalitarianism, in the face of which male and female, barbarian and cultured, slave and free, etc., are all of the same dignity.
- The process of binding and loosing, that is, deliberative morally accountable dialogue, dealing with offense and forgiveness (and thereby dealing with moral discernment), may recover the connection with forgiveness and with decision making which "church discipline" lost when it came to be tied with formal excommunication and the sanctions of hierarchical authority.

4. The minority church can be a foretaste of the peace for which the world was made. It is the function of minority communities to remember and to create utopian visions. There is no hope for society without an awareness of transcendence. Transcendence is not kept alive on the grounds of logical proof to the effect that there is a cosmos with a hereafter; but by the vitality of communities in which a different way of being keeps breaking in here and now. That we can really be led on a different way is the real proof of the transcendent power that offers hope of peace to the world as well. Nonconformity is the warrant for the promise of another world. In this world completely, the church nonetheless by its way of being represents the promise of another world, which is not somewhere else but which is to come here. That promissory quality of the church's present distinctiveness is making peace, as refusing to make war is its indispensable negative transcendence.

IF ONE IS IN CHRIST, THE WORLD IS NEW

The church cultivates an alternative consciousness. Another view of what the world is like is kept alive by narration and celebration which fly in the face of some of the "apparent" lessons of "realism."

1. The experience of isolation/oppression/suffering/powerlessness, when it is experienced together in a situation where joining the establishment is not possible morally, renews the community in its awareness that it is nonetheless worthwhile to go on living.

- There is the spirituality of "The Desert Is Fertile,"[12] and the long history of spiritual and material poverty as a respectable way to be human.
- There is learned empathy for others who are also victims—one learns to understand the power game from below and to see how different it looks from there.

2. A sign or a fruit of the creativity of the spirit is genuine innovation, surprise, and paradox in the ways one learns to see reality, as over against the monolinear "realism" of the established power system.

- One learns to trust in the power of weakness. There are some kinds of strength involved in being weak, or in accepting weakness, or in facing the facts that make one weak.
- One learns to see through the weakness of power. There are some kinds of apparent ability to achieve what one wills that constitute bondage, or an obstacle to genuine freedom to achieve what one thought one was able to do. With too large a weapon one cannot even reach one's enemies.

3. There is an alternative narrative. It is not simply that we tell stories and other people do not, although that is also often the case. The believing community has a longer sense of history past and future than do the oppressors. We also see the same facts differently. We do not assume that the only way to read national and political history is from the perspective of the winners. To remember that in every battle there was another side, and sometimes that there were more people on the other side and sometimes more worthy causes, sustains a different understanding of how we want to help history move.

The creative potential of narrative throws new light not only on the majority story. Also on "our side," things could have gone differently: we may discern in the minority experience absences of creativity or shortness of will, impatience or evil will, so that the story as it is told is a subject for repentance and not merely remembering; for making amends as well as for giving thanks. A repentant view of history is more creative than a eulogistic one.

4. There is ground for hoping when there is no *reason* to hope. In the Christian culture, both optimism and despair are correlated with the direct reading of how it is going for us in the rise and fall of power structures. The countercommunity reads these events otherwise, if not simply contrariwise. When things seem to be going well, we refuse to trust the rosiest promises, because we know how deeply imbedded in human optimism are the seeds of pride, and how easily when welcoming what we think to be good news we miss part of the picture and plan wrongly. When all seems to be going badly we do not abandon hope, not only because we have heard promises from beyond the system, but also because we have learned that sometimes our pessimistic readings of the present are shadowed by taking some setback too seriously.

It is then not merely a matter of occasionally having a perspective from which to see things differently: it is that we have a training ground for concretely expecting that things will usually be seen inadequately by those who read events from a posture of control. Thus we educate ourselves in the reasonable expectation that when we see things differently from others we will often be seeing them more truly. "Consciousness" is far more than a different set of ideas or assumptions; it is also style and skills. The minority community, through its ordinary social process and its rituals of reconciliation, through its dialogue and disputations, is an arena for training in conflict resolution and in the search for truth.

SERVANT STRENGTH

There are other ways to do Christian ethics than to ask "How can we move the total social system?" When Christians count among their number a monarch, or the majority in a democratic system, or a sizable and significant minority in a pluralistic democratic system, it is so natural as to be practically taken for granted that one way, perhaps *the* way to do moral deliberation, is to work out a consequentialist calculation of the direction one wants the whole social system to take. Seldom do people from within that heritage have occasion to stop to think that such calculation would be an irrelevant or at best utopian way of looking at things for a minority.

This is the particle of truth in the idea, given considerable currency since Max Weber, that an ethic of responsibility will be concerned with results from a given line of action, whereas an ethic of pure obedience will not care about effects. In that perspective it might even be taken as a sign of unfaithfulness to give as much attention as this study does to how the minority ethic "really works." Concern for effectiveness, we are told, is only fitting for those who can live up to that concern by actually managing the world. True obedience to suffering love must therefore presuppose the disavowal of concern for results. Seldom would the advocate of this pattern of division admit that it is based upon the establishment perspective. Only the person who believes that the "responsible use of power" from a position of domination is necessary in order to be useful will then presuppose that the alternative is moral purity at the price of ineffectiveness.

There may well be dimensions of effectiveness to a minority position even though its basic logic moves on other levels.

A minority group with no immediate chance of contributing to the way things go may still, by its dissent, maintain the wider community's awareness of some issues, in such a way that ideas which are unrealistic for the present may come to be credible later. This, for instance, was the American experience with Social Security. This innovation was quite unthinkable when first commended in 1930 by the American Socialist Norman Thomas. Later it became a possibility for a majority party to implement. Another way in which minority groups can contribute is to exercise pioneering creativity in places where no one is threatened and where they do jobs nobody else is interested in doing. Thereby they may gradually draw attention to some realm of social concern to which it would have been impossible to find an imposed solution. An example of this is the variety of recent exploratory visions developed by minority agencies in the realm of ministries to victims and offenders. The presence on the stage of a very different position, even though excluded as a possible model to be imposed by a majority, or negotiated by a sizable minority in a coalition situation, still does change the spectrum, and thereby moves its midpoint, and in the long run thus moves the balance point of the system.

Integrity and consistency are good policy in the long run, despite the fact that in the short run exceptions often seem to be justified. Quaker merchants in the eighteenth century progressed in merchandizing because of fair prices and good products, even though their prices were sometimes higher than others. Quakers as employers generally developed better relationships with employees. Even though better wages and employee rights represented an initial competitive disadvantage to the Quaker employer, these employers fostered worker involvement in management and initiated profit sharing. An edge in terms of quality work was the result.

The Protestant work ethic, although more demanding, also turns out to be more efficient in productivity for all parties involved. The conviction that one's morality and social style are expressive of a transcendent commitment, and not just of consequential calculation, itself contributes to the holding power of individuals in the face of short-range conflict and opposition, and forms a protection against resignation, a standard temptation to those whose reason for doing good is too closely correlated to manageable projections of effect. In a similar way, the support of a group is a complementary dimension of social reliability, which enables people to stand against the stream in the face of short-range effectiveness factors have time to work.

In yet one other way a morality based on principle has a special moral power. In most cultures there is some sort of public conscience or public opinion. Moral rhetoric has a kind of sacramental effect before the public at large, in both democratic and totalitarian cultures. The hard-nosed political realist can always say that moral rhetoric is not binding or convincing, yet generally it still tends to have some power of conviction to ordinary people. In the context of Anglo-Saxon democracy it has far more power than that, reaching in fact to the point where a Gandhi or a King or a Chavez can call forth a special new kind of social power by appealing symbolically to the idealism of the majority culture's rhetoric.

Once we have learned to step back from the preoccupation with the kind of measurement of effectiveness that expects results tomorrow by virtue of seizing control today, we learn to discern as well other kinds of "utility" which previously either were taken for granted without attention being given to them, or had been depreciated or ignored.

One thing that minorities learn to do is to survive: that is, to bequeath to later generations the alternative options for which there was no hearing this year or last. They can do this because the grounds for holding to what one holds have been conceived of in a way not dependent upon being ratified by present acclamation or success.

Whereas both democracy and demagoguery would have us believe that the course of events is determined by "the people" as a majority, social and political realism know that most societies are sufficiently divided that under the surface the reality of decision processes, even in totalitarian countries, is a matter of bargaining and brokering among factions. A minority faith community is more able than those factions whose identity is determined only by ideology or only by group interest to maintain a strong bargaining posture in such a mix. The advantage of American life is that faction politics, especially in our major metropolitan centers, in principle, is out in the open, so we can see that some groups do their negotiating shrewdly and others clumsily. The faith community has both the cultural and normative resources to make that factional bargaining constructive and honest, and the internal cohesion to keep its leaders accountable and its bargaining goals realistic. A faith community differs as well from other pressure groups in that without denying an element of self-centered bias and interest it is able to claim that its social goals are in the interest of others. This is dramatically visible for the Quaker involvement in corrections and abolition in early America or for the Jewish involvement in civil liberties in our time.

I have already identified above the way in which a minority community can appeal to the conscience of society at large and call it to outdo itself occasionally in moral commitment. The other way in which a minority can be the conscience of the society is to continue to voice the claims of unrepresented peoples and causes, when they do not yet have the ear or the heart of the majority. My individual conscience may tell me that I am doing wrong even when I am not sure what would be the right thing to do. It may maintain my malaise so that my search for a not-yet-visible solution will not be abandoned or short-circuited. The minority presence as conscience of society works in a similar way, as can be seen at present in the field of corrections. Insightful minorities are telling our society that what we are doing with offenders is counterproductive, even when no one has the outlines of a better solution. If truth were left to a market philosophy, there would be no point in continuing to make an argument for which there are no takers or to ask a question for which there are no answers. The minority community has other grounds to sustain that wholesome discomfort, and thereby keeps the door open for solutions not yet found. Paradoxical though it seems, a position which is not justified on the grounds of calculating effectiveness will turn out in the long run to be more effective than one which at every step along the way is the object of a cost/benefit calculation. This position rejects some ways of deriving ethics from calculations of effectiveness, yet represents commitment to, not against, long and broad usefulness.

LET IT BE

The next category of description could possibly be labeled "acquiescence." Minority perspective makes the vocabulary of moral evaluation more nuanced. This is one of the points of most difficulty in dialogue between majority and minority people. In a majority situation the normal expression of "responsibility," by those who hold power, and who believe they have been given it by God, is to work to approximate a coincidence between what is right and what really happens. Right behavior is sanctioned positively, wrong behavior is sanctioned negatively, with the degree of rigor depending on the size of the offense and the degree of need to prevent it or compensate for it. The only elements left unregulated are those concerning which there is either honest ignorance or acceptable difference of opinion, or concerning which no means of enforcement can be found proportionate to the stakes. In this situation, then, any morally aware person, being presumed to be associated with the majority that has power, is in some accessory sense responsible (i.e., accountable) for everything that happens. To let something happen by inaction is practically as grave as to do it oneself, since it is presumed that one could have stopped it. To let something happen is morally the same as doing it oneself. Not stopping Hitler is the same as helping him.

The entire landscape looks different from a position of weakness. If you could not have stopped something, then you are not in the same way to blame when it happens. The rest of a Pandora's box of differences arises from this distinction. No longer do we simply have the two categories of "right," which we must foster or even enforce, and "wrong," which we must prohibit and punish. Between the clean categories a host of other gradations arise. These are not the same as the moral gradations in the (Reinhold) Niebuhrian scheme, where the persons who are responsible find their unselfishness mixed with self-interest and their servanthood to others diluted with pragmatic realism: that is still a modulation of doing the morally right thing.

In a situation of majority control, if something happens it is because you let it happen and you are to blame for it, even for the things you recognize have some disadvantages. Reinhold Niebuhr was more frank than his predecessors about the fact that some of the things you believe you have to do, some of the hard choices you have to take responsibility for, are in themselves harmful or hurtful to others and are to some degree selfish. Nonetheless he still was able to claim that on balance that particular expression of hurtfulness and selfishness was the best available possibility. It is the best available possibility for the sake of the whole community, and it is therefore a positive expression of moral responsibility to use whatever violence, joined with whatever self-interest is necessary in order to bring about the least evil outcome.

The weak know that there are things one cannot prevent that are not right. There are sins which it is not possible or desirable to treat as crimes, even if one had the kind of majority status that would permit the making of the laws. The major recent American experience in this respect was with Prohibition. There are also voices today suggesting that drug abuse, like adult homosexuality and heterosexual adultery, like most of the other deadly sins (gluttony, sloth, avarice, pride, . . .) could not properly be dealt with in the courts even if there were a majority to declare them worthy of civil punishment.

There are things we cannot control, which nonetheless are going to happen, which are going to impinge upon the situation where we are ourselves trying to do something else. This means that it will be an expression of wisdom, and not of self-righteousness or unconcern or isolation, if we accept the fact that those deeds are going to be done and that we cannot stop them. One of the differences weakness makes is that the powerless have thought more about the fact that there are evils one cannot prevent.

The entire calculation of responsibilities is utterly different in a situation where one has no capacity to impose one's preference. The situation being decisively controlled by other powers, one does the best one can to serve what can be served and save what can be saved in a bad situation. In that context most pacifists accept the fact that nonpacifists will be running the world violently, and interlock their own rejection of violence with the knowledge that others will keep on killing and coercing. The reckoning of what it takes to bring about desired results is disconnected from realistic short-term measurements of feasibility. Instead of asking about one's action "If I do this how will it tip the scale?" one rather asks "In a situation where I cannot tip the scales, on what other grounds might I decide what to do?"

BACK TO TRUE NORTH

The imperatives of dialogue with majority mentalities have skewed this description toward the problematic of weakness and effectiveness. An authentic portrayal of the peace church vision from the inside would have spoken instead of worship and servanthood, reconciliation and creativity, heartfelt religion and transforming hope, and the person of Jesus Christ. The reader could have asked why any of that should be considered "sectarian."

NOTES

1. The phrase "historic peace churches" seems to have become current first in the mid-1930s in the U.S., as Brethren, Friends, and Mennonites saw the need to band together in the light of the new threat of war.

2. A fuller presentation of this argument was presented in "The 'Constantinian' Sources of Western Social Ethics," in *The Priestly Kingdom* (Notre Dame, Ind.: University of Notre Dame Press, 1985), 135ff. One of the earliest formulations of this way of seeing the problem was Paul Peachey's "New Ethical Possibility: The Task of 'Post-Christendom' Ethics," *Interpretation*, vol. 19, no. 1 (January 1965): 26–38.

3. The reference to Constantine in the following exposition has a code function. The first Roman emperor to tolerate, and then to favor, and finally to participate in the administration of the Christian churches is the symbol of a shift in relationships which had begun before he came on the scene and was not completed until nearly a century after his death. Although his thoughts and his deeds are eminently representative of the nature of the shift, it is not our present concern to discharge the task of the historian, to interpret the man by asking questions about his sincerity or his wisdom or his relative causative importance. The symbolic value of Constantine as representative of that change was not an invention of his critics or of Christian radicals either in the twelfth century or more recently. It was rather the adulatory historians of the school of Eusebius of Caesarea who gave to his age and to his person that dramatic centrality. Radical histo-

rians argued that the change was not all for the good, whereas "mainstream" theologians from Augustine to Bullinger and Bucer saw him as initiator of the millennium.

4. The more methodologically self-aware ethical systems use the phrases "sphere sovereignty" and "Eigengesetzlichkeit der Kulturgebiete."

5. Cf. in my *Original Revolution* (Scottdale, Pa.: Herald Press, 1972) the treatment of "the other lights" (pp. 134ff.). It is the merit of the age of Reinhold Niebuhr to have made this tension clear.

6. Cf. my "Anabaptism and History" in *The Priestly Kingdom*, 123ff.

7. The interlock of complementary ministries is detailed in my text "The Hermeneutic of Peoplehood," in ibid., 15ff.

8. *The Church Against the World* (Chicago: Willett, Clarke & Co., 1935), 1, 123ff.

9. *Christian Ethics and Social Policy* (New York: Charles Scribner's Sons, 1946), 90–91.

10. His postretirement work, *The Radical Imperative* (Philadelphia: Westminster Press, 1975), deals with ideas, not with their social shape.

A powerful parallel witness to such writings as those of H. Richard Niebuhr and Bennett, cited above, was offered two generations later by Julian N. Hartt, in his *A Christian Critique of American Culture* (New York: Harper & Row, 1967). The phrase "culture Christianity," used to name what Hartt is critiquing, has a meaning similar to that in the H. Richard Niebuhr volume thirty-three years before: Hartt's critical analysis is far more complex. His description of the church (esp. pp. 292ff.) is likewise more complex, in the way it characterizes the interaction between what the community of believers is called to be and what it is: not much more is said about concrete directions for the life of real communities which might incarnate ("inculturate") a critique like Hartt's.

11. Cf. Robert Tucker, "Revolutionary Faithfulness," in Martin E. Marty and Dean G. Peerman, eds., *New Theology*, no. 6 (New York: Macmillan Co., 1969), 204, and Wolfgang Schäufele, *Das missionarische Bewusstsein und Wirken der Täufer* (Neukirchen: Neukirchener Verlag, 1966).

12. Title of the devotional work of Dom Helder Camara (Maryknoll, N.Y.: Orbis Books, 1982).

6

MORAL DISCOURSE
ABOUT WAR IN THE
EARLY CHURCH

JAMES F. CHILDRESS

INTRODUCTION

I want to examine two elements of the moral discourse about war in the early church up to and including Augustine: first, the moral pressures toward the justification of Christian participation in war, and, second, the strategies of restricting the range or reducing the weight of the precepts (especially in the Sermon on the Mount) that appeared to rule out participation in war. I will concentrate on ideas rather than on other pressures and forces in the situation of the church in Roman society. This concentration does not presuppose that ideas were the dominant forces in the changes that occurred in the early church. Practice may have led the way, as Adolf Harnack suggests,[1] but moral discourse about war was also important, at least in legitimating Christian participation in war and in reducing the tensions between the precepts of the Sermon on the Mount and service in war. I will use some contemporary philosophical categories to illuminate early Christian discourse. The historical evidence regarding early Christian practice and attitudes is worthy of attention first, however.

Until A.D. 170–80 there is no direct evidence that Christians participated in military service or that they abstained from such service. For various reasons it is probable that few Christians were soldiers. Celsus criticized Christians for not serving in the army, but there is evidence from A.D. 170–80 that some Christians were in the army.[2] Their numbers increased in subsequent decades.

James F. Childress, a member of the Society of Friends, is Commonwealth Professor of Religious Studies and professor of medical education at the University of Virginia in Charlottesville. Among his other writings on war and peace is *Moral Responsibility in Conflicts: Essays on Nonviolence, War, and Conscience* (Baton Rouge: Louisiana State University Press, 1982).

In what sense was the early church *pacifist,* if it was? As "making peace," pacifism may be defined by any particular proponent to include various positive attitudes and activities. But a minimal definition of pacifism is *opposition to war and/or to participation in war.* Several commentators have identified the stance of the early church as one of "anti-militarism," "nonviolence," or "conscientious objection," frequently using these terms interchangeably.[3] Certainly the church opposed "militarism" even when it recognized the legitimacy of war, and it opposed "violence" even though it did not adopt a method of nonviolence in the contemporary sense.[4] Because a number of Christians were soldiers, at least after 170 A.D., and because the church did not excommunicate them, it would be impossible to describe the attitudes and activities of the church as "conscientious objection," a phrase that appropriately describes the stance of such Christians as Maximilian (who will be discussed below). Nevertheless, Christian writers tended to oppose Christian participation in war even when they accepted the institution of war. Roland Bainton's comment is apt: "The age of persecution down to the time [of] Constantine was the *age of pacifism* to the degree that during this period no Christian author to our knowledge approved of Christian participation in battle."[5]

Even if Christian writers were "pacifist" in the minimal sense that they opposed Christian participation in war through military service, their grounds for "pacifism" included such diverse reasons as opposition to Rome as a persecutor, anticipation of a speedy end to earthly society, fear of idolatry and divided loyalties in military service (especially the *sacramentum*), immoral practices of soldiers, and aversion to bloodshed.[6] Modern analysts contend that all these reasons but the last one are essentially "non-pacifistic" and that, insofar as these reasons were offered, opposition to participation in war was not "pacifistic," even though it satisfies our minimal definition. Nevertheless, in the Christian opposition to participation in war aversion to bloodshed was important and required attention even after the other reasons for opposing military service became obsolete because of Christianity's dominant role. This aversion to bloodshed can be seen also in the opposition to viewing gladiatorial games, to viewing and participating in executions (even by testifying in a criminal trial), and to homicide.[7] This aversion to bloodshed persisted in some of the attitudes of later writers toward killing even in just wars. Without exploring the theological-moral reasons for this aversion to bloodshed here, at the very least, it is clear that it is grounded in the requirement of neighbor-love and buttressed by various theological convictions such as the eschatological role of Christians.[8]

Early Christian writers tended to think about military service in *pastoral* terms, especially whether soldiers who converted to Christianity could remain in military service.[9] In their concern for the relation of the Christian to the Roman Empire, these writers did not develop general theories about governments, war, and the justification of war. Although they criticized several military practices, especially those having to do with religion, their general perspective (hardly a theory) on government recognized the legitimacy of lethal coercion in both its internal and external manifestations. In their *apologetic* tasks, several Christian writers, such as Origen, articulated general principles regarding Christian participation in society at large, but even they stopped short of indicating the conditions of just war for the guidance of non-Christians. While they recognized the legitimacy of war and the military profession—though not for Christians—they did not develop a framework for assessing wars. The rudiments of such a framework appear, in part under the influence of Stoic thought, in the writings of Ambrose and Augustine.

ARGUMENTS FOR PARTICIPATION IN WAR

One major pressure toward the justification of participation in war came from the very principle that supported pacifism: the principle of love. In order to identify the tensions created by the principle of love itself, I will draw on William Frankena's analysis of beneficence (which early Christians considered to be a part, though not necessarily all, of love). Frankena distinguishes four levels of beneficence:[10]

1. One ought *not to inflict* evil or harm (what is bad) [sometimes called nonmaleficence];
2. One ought to *prevent* evil or harm;
3. One ought to *remove* evil;
4. One ought to do or *promote* good.

"Evil" or "harm" can be defined as damage to an *interest*. While persons have many interests, I will focus here on the interest in physical integrity and survival. "Violence" or, in the language of the early church, "bloodshed" is a clear "evil" or "harm" because it damages a person's interests. Whatever else love or beneficence requires, it certainly prohibits the *infliction* of evil or harm, including bloodshed. Christian pacifists affirmed the priority and absoluteness of beneficence 1. For example, in 295 Maximilian was liable for military service because he was the son of a veteran of the Roman army. When he was called up for military service at age twenty-one, he refused to serve, saying: "I cannot serve as a soldier; I cannot do evil; I am a Christian" ("Non possum militare, non possum malefacere—

Christianus sum").[11] He was executed. In 298 Marcellus, a centurion, objected to pagan sacrifices and to shedding blood: "I threw down [my arms]; for it was not seemly that a Christian man, who renders military service to the Lord Christ, should render it [also] by [inflicting] earthly injuries."[12]

Thus, many Christians believed that beneficence 1 had priority over beneficences 2 through 4. How could the use of lethal force against X be construed as beneficent when, at the very least, it violates beneficence 1? Christians faced several conflicts in trying to apply the principle of love. First, what does love require when my interests come into conflict with another person's interests? Second, what does love require when the interests of two different neighbors conflict, perhaps because X is attacking Y? Third, what does love require when my definition of my neighbor's interests conflicts with that neighbor's definition of his or her own interests? None of these conflicts could be resolved by reference to the parable of the Good Samaritan.

Regarding the first conflict, Christians generally held, even after the acceptance of participation in war, that they should not use lethal force to protect their own individual interests in situations of self-defense or necessity (e.g., the Christian and another person swimming toward a board after a shipwreck). The Christian should be willing to sacrifice himself or herself. But the duty of love to *prevent or remove* evil or harm could justify the use of lethal force in the second conflict, for example, when X is attacking Y who is innocent. Love may not be able to meet the needs of all the parties in a conflict; in order to protect the innocent party, it may have to use physical force. The resolution of this second conflict may presuppose standards of justice in order to determine which party is innocent and which is guilty, and it often presupposes a public role or authorization. Before analyzing this second conflict in more detail, I want to note that while the third conflict usually raises questions of paternalism in other settings, Augustine contended that in the use of lethal force the target could also be a beneficiary. As Frederick Russell interprets Augustine, "the just warrior restrained sinners from evil, thus acting against their will but in their own best interest."[13]

Augustine claimed that what is wrong for the Christian is not military service as such but the malice that often accompanies it ("Non enim beneficere prohibet militia, sed malitia").[14] In preventing or removing evil or harm, such as X's attack on Y, the Christian does not violate beneficences 2 through 4 even though he or she violates beneficence 1. Thus, beneficence, broadly conceived, does not prohibit all infliction of harms; it may permit infliction of harm and even bloodshed under some circumstances. This argument does not, however, *require* infliction of harm by Christians.

A second moral pressure toward justification of Christian participation came from a recognition of responsibility for harms and evils inflicted by others. While this second point is an extension of the first point, it merits separate treatment. Its most dramatic statement appears in Ambrose's discussion of the virtue of fortitude.

> The glory of fortitude, therefore, does not rest only on the strength of one's body or of one's arms, but rather on the courage of the mind. Nor is the law of courage exercised in causing, *but in driving away all harm. He who does not keep harm off a friend, if he can, is as much in fault as he who causes it.* Wherefore holy Moses gave this as a first proof of his fortitude in war. For when he saw a Hebrew receiving hard treatment at the hands of an Egyptian, he defended him, and laid low the Egyptian and hid him in the sand. Solomon also says: "Deliver him that is led to death."[15]

Obviously much of this passage shows the courage or fortitude involved in preventing or removing harm or evil—the second and third features of beneficence—even when it is necessary to inflict harm or evil. But it contains an even stronger argument: "He who does not keep harm off a friend, if he can, is as much in fault as he who causes it" ("Qui non repellit a socio injuriam, si potest, tam est in vitio quam ille qui facit").[16] Ambrose's claim presupposes judgments about the justice of one party in a conflict, and he insists that the virtue of courage "never stands alone," but requires justice: "in matters of war, one ought to see whether the war is just or unjust." For Ambrose, failures of beneficences 2 through 4 may also be failures of justice, as Cicero had written: "There are two kinds of injustice—the one, on the part of those who inflict wrong, the other on the part of those who, when they can, do not shield from wrong those upon whom it is being inflicted."[17] Thus, a failure to realize beneficences 2 and 3 for Y when X is unjustly harming Y is itself unjust and not merely a violation of love.

There is another way to state this point about responsibility: there is no moral difference between killing Y and letting Y be killed when we have the power to prevent Y's death. Agents bear responsibility for states of affairs, not only for what they do. This issue of outcomes or consequences appears at every stage of debates about appropriate actions or means in the contemporary context: (a) nonresistance, (b) nonviolent resistance, (c) violence (within limits), (d) unlimited violence (such as indiscriminate attacks on noncombatants in war).[18] The argument for moving from one action to another usually takes the same form: the relation of means and ends or the relation of actions and outcomes. Is it legitimate to use some means to bring

about a good outcome or to avoid a bad outcome? Giving priority to beneficence 1, the pacifist such as Maximilian draws the line for means at (a) or
(b), saying "non possum malefacere." The just warrior such as Ambrose
insists that beneficence 2 toward Y may take priority over beneficence 1
toward X (i.e., nonmaleficence toward X) when X is harming Y, because
nonintervention would violate justice as well as beneficence 2. For the just
warrior, a doctrine of negative responsibility, that is, responsibility for the
consequences of what others do, becomes central.[19]

A third moral pressure toward justification of Christian participation in
war can be stated as the generalization test, or the fairness test, which was
posed most sharply for early Christians, as far as our records go, by Celsus,
the second-century critic. Celsus asked Christians to consider what would
happen if everyone did what they were doing. He contended that *"if everyone were to do the same as you,* there would be nothing to prevent him [the
emperor] from being abandoned, alone and deserted, while earthly things
would come into the power of the most lawless and savage barbarians, and
nothing more would be heard among men either of your worship or of the
true wisdom" (Origen *Contra Celsum* 8.68).[20]

This argument was presented in the context of the duty to give the
emperor his due, including military service. Celsus was also quoted as saying (8.55):

> Reason demands one of two alternatives. If they refuse to worship in the
> proper way the lords in charge of the following activities, then they ought
> neither to come to the estate of a free man, nor to marry a wife, nor to beget
> children, nor to do anything else in life. But they should depart from this
> world leaving no descendants at all behind them, so that such a race would
> entirely cease to exist on earth. But if they are going to marry wives, and
> beget children, and taste of the fruits, and partake of the joys of this life,
> and endure the appointed evils (by nature's law all men must have experi-
> ence of evils; evil is necessary and has nowhere else to exist), then they
> ought to render the due honours to the beings who have been entrusted
> with these things. And they ought to offer the due rites of worship in this
> life until they are set free from their bonds, lest they even appear ungrateful
> to them. It is wrong for people to partake of what is their property to offer
> them nothing in return.

Another translation of the last sentence is "It is unfair to take a share in the
goods that the emperor possesses and not to contribute anything for
them."[21]

"If everyone were to do the same as you . . . ?" Or "What would happen
if everyone did that?" Such questions are sometimes dismissed in moral

discourse as unsophisticated, but Origen quite rightly perceived their moral significance and tried to answer them. Indeed, Celsus's question identified a fundamental moral problem for Christians and required a strong answer, an even stronger answer than Origen could manage. One of the moral prerequisites for justifying refusal of military service is that it pass what I will call the generalization test, often identified by the question, "But what if everyone did that?" This test is connected with what Marcus Singer, a contemporary philosopher, calls the generalization argument: "If everyone were to do that, the consequences would be disastrous (or undesirable); therefore, no one ought to do that." The generalization argument itself presupposes what Singer calls the generalization principle: "What is right (or wrong) for one person must be right (or wrong) for any similar person in similar circumstances."[22] According to many philosophers, this generalization principle (sometimes called the principle of universalizability) is presupposed by moral judgments.

It is tempting to respond to the question "If everyone were to do the same . . ." by insisting that "not everyone will." This sort of response can be seen in John Howard Yoder's writings: "The most frequent response to the initial peace testimony of Christian pacifists is, 'What would happen if everybody did this?' Since we are all children of Christendom we think we must answer this; but logically we need not and cannot—because everyone will not."[23] Yoder responds to the generalization test by an *empirical* prediction: not everyone will do what the Christian pacifist does. Origen did not treat the question of generalization in this way, but several commentators have argued that his response to Celsus makes sense only if Christians can be expected to be a *minority* in the world.[24] Perhaps even Celsus's observation regarding Christians partially expresses this point: "If all men wanted to be Christians, the Christians would no longer want them" (3.9). Origen actually believed that the world was being converted to Christianity and that he could recommend that all people do just the same as he because (1) in a Christian world there would be no lethal conflict, and (2) a large number of Christians in the Roman Empire before the conversion of the barbarians would be able to save the empire by their prayers.

Let *all men do just the same* as I. Let them deny the Homeric doctrine, while keeping the doctrine of the divine right of the king and observing the command "Honour the king." Yet on such a basis as this neither would the emperor be left alone, nor would he be deserted, nor would earthly things be in the power of the most lawless and savage barbarians. For if, as Celsus has it, everyone would to do the same as I, obviously the barbarians would also be converted to the word of God and would be the most law-abiding and mild. And all other worship would be done away and only that of the Christians would prevail. One day it will be the only one to prevail, since the word is continually gaining possession of more souls. (*Contra Celsum* 8.68)

Such an argument obviously depends on beliefs about moral sanctification after conversion.

Even if only Romans became Christians—not the whole world—the Roman Empire would still survive because of the power of Christian prayers. Celsus had noted that it would be difficult for Christians to rely on God for protection, without any other defense, for God had let the Jews down when they had relied on him: "Instead of being masters of the whole world, they have been left no land or home of any kind" (8.69). Origen responded that God's promises are contingent on keeping the law, and that Jews had not kept the law and had committed a "crime against Jesus."

> However, if as Celsus suggests all the Romans were convinced and praised, they would be superior to their enemies, or would not even fight wars at all, since they would be protected by divine power which is reported to have preserved five entire cities for the sake of fifty righteous men. For the men of God are the salt of the world, preserving the permanence of things on earth, and earthly things hold together so long as the salt does not turn bad. (8.70)

Origen also partially dealt with the generalization test when he responded to Celsus's exhortation to Christians to "help the emperor with all our power, and cooperate with him in what is right, and fight for him, and be fellow-soldiers if he presses for this, and fellow-generals with him." This argument is closely connected with the generalization test, because it requires a specification, a fuller description, of "What if everyone did *that?*" or "If everyone were to do the *same*. . . ." *What* are Christians doing that may not be generalizable? The description of the action is important because the test depends on whether Christians are "not bearing their fair share of the burdens," "not serving the emperor," or "not accepting military service." Origen tried to show that refusal of military service is not unfair because Christians serve the emperor more effectively in other ways:

> at appropriate times we render to the emperors divine help, if I may so say, by taking up even the whole armour of God. And this we do in obedience to the apostolic utterance which says: "I exhort you, therefore, first to make prayers, supplications, intercessions, and thanksgivings for all men, for emperors, and all that are in authority." Indeed, the more pious a man is, the more effective he is in helping the emperors—more so than the soldiers who go out into the lines and kill all the enemy troops that they can. (8.73)

Christians are of "more help to the emperors than those who seem to be doing the fighting" because Christians by prayers "destroy all daemons which stir up wars, violate oaths, and disturb the peace." They "fight on behalf of the emperor." "Even though we do not become fellow-soldiers with him, even if he presses for this, yet we are fighting for him and composing a special army of piety through our intercessions to God" (8.73). This theme of *militia Christi* was widespread in the early church.[25] Not only did the military provide a natural metaphor, despite the Christian revulsion to bloodshed, but it served important rhetorical purposes in moral discourse, as Origen's response to Celsus suggests. Christians are "fighting on behalf of the emperor," even if they serve only in the *militia Christi*, not in the militia of Rome. They render an alternative but more necessary and efficacious service.[26] In short, in contemporary language, they recognized an *obligation to the government*, but not an *obligation to perform military service*. They claimed discretion about the nature of their service.

"We who offer prayers with righteousness, together with ascetic practices and exercises which teach us to despise pleasures and not to be led by them, are cooperating in the tasks of the community" (8.73). Indeed, even though they are not soldiers or generals, Christians "do more good to their countries than the rest of mankind, since they educate the citizens and teach them to be devoted to God, the guardian of their city . . ." (8.74). The importance of the description of *what* Christians are doing is evident in Origen's claim that "If Christians do avoid these responsibilities [of public office], it is not with the motive of shirking the public services of life. But they keep themselves for a more divine and necessary service in the church of God for the sake of the salvation of men" (8.75).

But insofar as Origen appealed not only to Christians' contribution to the good of the salvation of men, but also to their contribution to the goods of the earthly city, he tried to indicate that the principle at work was already recognized by Celsus and fellow Romans. It is customary, Origen noted, for the Romans to exempt their "priests of certain images and wardens of the temples of the gods" from military service in order to keep their right hands undefiled for the sake of sacrifices. "If, then, this is reasonable, how much more reasonable is it that, while others fight, Christians also should be fighting as priests and worshippers of God, keeping their right hands pure and by their prayers to God striving for those who fight in a righteous cause and for the emperor who reigns righteously, in order that everything which is opposed and hostile to those who act rightly may be destroyed?" (8.73). At this point, Origen appears to presuppose minority status for

Christians; at any rate, his attempt to make the Christian nonparticipation reasonable probably depends on late Neoplatonic spirituality with its idea of gradation; the masses are distinguished from the elite who perform indispensable tasks for the whole but not the same tasks as the masses.[27]

What made Origen's position difficult to maintain was the recognition of the justification of the institution of war in a fallen world. Indeed, as Cecil John Cadoux notes, throughout the early church there was a "relative justification of war."[28] War as an institution was recognized as justified and even necessary in a fallen world and, in principle, some wars were recognized as just. Origen admitted that the spread of Christianity depended on the *Pax Romana* and that the *Pax Romana* depended on the use of lethal force (2.30). But the relative justification of war, recognition of some wars as just, and appreciation of the *Pax Romana* were combined with a denial of the legitimacy of Christian participation in war; this denial was apparently accepted by many ordinary Christians and supported by most Christian thinkers until the fourth century. The Christian refusal to bear arms in war, however, was also combined with a willingness to pray for the emperor's success in war. Indeed, these prayers, along with other contributions to the society, were viewed as alternative service, even more efficacious and necessary than bearing arms. As Christianity spread and threats to the *Pax Romana* continued and increased, it was predictably harder to justify Christian participation only by prayer rather than through killing in conflict, especially under a Christian emperor. Trust in God through prayer was supplemented by efforts to control the outcome through the use of force under the authority of the government. Because participation in war continued to be in tension with important moral and religious convictions, it is important to see how several Christian thinkers handled this tension in their moral discourse about war.

STRATEGIES OF ACCOMMODATION

LeRoy Walters has identified four questions that just-war theories attempt to answer: Whether war can be just? When? Who may fight? How may war be fought?[29] The first three questions can be seen in relation to three strands of the most *stringent* interpretation of such sayings in the Sermon on the Mount as "turn the other cheek" and "go the second mile." According to the most stringent interpretation, these sayings are to be taken as *literal, absolute,* and *universal.* They would thus literally rule out any physical force, including warfare, under any conditions by anyone, whether Christian or not. Such a stringent interpretation has rarely been accepted by Christian pacifists. While Leo Tolstoy (1828–1910), the great

Russian novelist who embraced a radical Christian nonresistance, may be a modern exception, no one in the early church, to my knowledge, accepted these sayings in all three ways—as literal, absolute, and universal—though Lactantius may have come close. While most Christian writers apparently viewed these demands as absolute, that is, as unconditionally binding, only a few took them literally, and most restricted their range of application by applying them only to Christians. As we have seen, one reason for restricting the range of these demands was a broader interpretation of the principle of love that undergirded them.

It is important to distinguish the *scope* from the *strength* or the *range* from the *force* of moral concepts. It is possible, for example, to hold that a moral rule is absolutely binding within a limited range of circumstances or for a limited number of people with special characteristics. Because prohibition of violence (beneficence 1) was absolute for Christians, they could not participate in warfare, but non-Christians were not subject to this prohibition. Thus, early Christian pacifists accepted a dualism between Christians and the world, acknowledging "the relative justification of war" for the world at large in view of the necessity of coercive government in God's plan for fallen humanity.[30]

As Christian participation in war became accepted, the church and its theologians developed ways other than the church/world dichotomy to restrict the range or the force of the New Testament demands, thereby reducing, but not eliminating, the tension experienced by Christians. These include (but are not limited to) the following:

- Higher/lower
- For oneself/for others
- Inner/outer
- Private/public

For just-war theorists, sayings from the Sermon on the Mount applied only to the first item of each pair. These distinctions are not, of course, mutually exclusive; they were often combined, for example, by Augustine.

Higher / Lower

While distinction between *higher* and *lower* standards of conduct appeared in the distinction between church and world, it became significantly different when it was applied *within* the church or *among* Christians. Two levels of morality became accepted as legitimate for Christians: Some Christians could participate in war (indeed, by 416 only Christians could be soldiers), while other Christians were barred from participation (indeed, even ex-soldiers could not become priests).[31] According to Eusebius of Caesarea, Constantine's bishop and advisor, there were two levels of

Christian vocation: lay people could participate in just wars, marry, etc., while clergy could not participate (by bearing arms) in just wars, could not marry, etc.[32] The standards for the clergy were "above nature, and beyond common human living."[33] According to Ambrose, "the thought of warlike matters seems to be foreign to the duty of our office [as clergy], for we have our thoughts fixed more on the duty of the soul than on that of the body, nor is it our business to look to arms but rather to the forces of peace."[34] This distinction between levels of Christian morality (including precepts and counsels) and vocation appeared in at least sketchy form in writings by Clement and by Chrysostom; it was developed more fully by such medieval theologians as Thomas. It also has analogues in Judaism.[35]

For Oneself/For Others

Even for ordinary Christians judged by lower standards of morality, the sayings such as "turn the other cheek" and the principles of love and beneficence had moral relevance, though they did not preclude participation in war. For example, there was an important distinction between *motives* for the use of force, and the demands of the Sermon on the Mount were held to permit some motives while excluding others: While it became permissible to use force for the sake of others, it was not permissible to use force for one's own sake. Ambrose appealed to this distinction in situations of necessity and self-defense. In discussing the problem of the so-called board of Carneades, he noted that

> some ask whether a wise man ought in case of a shipwreck to take away a plank from an ignorant sailor? Although it seems better for the common good that a wise man rather than a fool should escape from shipwreck, yet I do not think that a Christian, a just and wise man, ought to save his own life by the death of another; *just as when he meets with an armed robber he cannot return his blows, lest in defending his life he should stain his love toward his neighbour.* The verdict on this is plain and clear in the books of the Gospel. "Put up thy sword, for every one that taketh the sword shall perish with the sword." What robber is more hateful than the persecutor who came to kill Christ? But Christ would not be defended from the wounds of the persecutor, for He willed to heal all by His wounds.[36]

Augustine also accepted this distinction between motives:

> As to killing others to defend one's own life I do not approve of this, unless one happen to be a soldier or a public functionary acting not for himself, but in defense of others or of the city in which he resides.[37]

The motivation of acting for others could include killing X in order to protect Y, or in order to benefit X himself or herself, or in order to deter others from harming innocent persons. These other-directed benefits could be intended in the same act. As Augustine noted,

> For as it is not benevolent to give a man help at the expense of some greater benefit he might receive, so it is not innocent to spare a man at the risk of his falling into graver sin. To be innocent, we must not only do harm to no man, but also restrain him from sin or punish his sin, so that either the man himself who is punished may profit by his experience, or others be warned by his example.[38]

Inner / Outer

The distinction between inner and outer is closely related to the previous distinction between types of motives. This third distinction, which emphasizes the importance of motives and dispositions in action, may even be presupposed by the second distinction, but it merits separate treatment because of its full and systematic statement by Augustine, who developed it in opposition to claims that the precepts of the Sermon on the Mount are to be taken literally. Augustine offered a *reductio ad absurdum* argument regarding the precept about turning the other cheek. He noted that Jesus had identified the "right cheek," but that most people are right-handed and thus would tend to strike people on their left cheek. Therefore, according to Augustine, Jesus' "precepts pertain rather to the inward disposition of the heart than to the actions which are done in the sight of men, requiring us, in the inmost heart, to cherish patience along with benevolence, but in the outward action to do that which seems most likely to benefit those whose good we ought to seek. . . ." The real evils in war are attitudinal, not physical, for the people killed would have soon died in any case. "The real evils in war are love of violence, revengeful cruelty, fierce and implacable enmity, wild resistance, and the lust of power, and such like. . . ." Wars should aim to punish such evils, as well as to seek peace, the object of war. Even in waging war, agents should "cherish the spirit of a peacemaker."[39] Wars should thus be fought out of "necessity," under the authorization of the state or God, not out of revenge. Good people in war should experience regret, if not remorse; they should experience "grief" and "mental pain" because of war's miseries. Even if war is just, it is, nonetheless, mournful.

Russell correctly observes that "the suspicion of all killing in war continued to nip at the heels of the just war theories."[40] In the fifth century, Isidore of Pelusium declared that "private murders are impure and guilty. But there is no guilt in killing in a just war." Nevertheless, he noted that in Mosaic law soldiers had to isolate and purify themselves after battle, observing that "if we examine thoroughly the indisputable blood relationship which exists between all mankind, they are not without sin, either."[41] Earlier Basil the Great had contended that although "our fathers" differentiated killing in war from murder, "perhaps it would be well that those whose hands are unclean abstain from communion for three years."[42]

Private / Public

The fourth distinction is between *private* and *public* actions, especially between actions undertaken by a person without public authorization and actions undertaken by a person with public authorization. In private actions precepts such as "turn the other cheek" apply, but in public actions other standards apply. In part, this distinction deals with both *when* war may be fought and *who* may fight. As Augustine developed this distinction, war is just only when it is fought under divine or governmental authorization. Rebellion has no place. When Jesus said that "he who takes the sword shall perish by the sword" he referred to those who are not authorized to use the sword. "To take the sword is to use weapons against a man's life, without the sanction of the constituted authority."[43] Within public roles, both superiors and subordinates can describe their actions as necessary for public safety and hence without sin.

According to Ambrose and Augustine, among others, authorization is only one of several criteria of just wars, but for the ordinary Christian subject it probably was the most important criterion. In an unjust war, the soldier "may do the duty belonging to his position in the State in fighting by the order of his sovereign—for in some cases it is plainly the will of God that he should fight, and in others, where this is not so plain, it may be an unrighteous command on the part of the king, while the soldier is innocent, because his position makes obedience a duty. . . ."[44]

I have examined some of the moral and theological convictions that created tensions for early Christians who affirmed that the government's sword is ordained by God for a fallen world but that Christians should not exercise it in war. Three important pressures toward Christian participation in war were (1) the recognition that love requires preventing or removing harm as well as not inflicting harm, (2) the related sense of responsibility, fault, and guilt for omissions, and (3) the generalization test as proposed by Celsus. Along with many other factors, these ideas contributed to the legitimation of Christian participation in war. But such legitimation itself created additional tensions, particularly because of the requirements of the Sermon on the Mount to "love your enemies," "to turn the other cheek," "to go the second mile," etc. In order to lessen these tensions, the church and its theologians developed several interrelated distinctions that could restrict the scope of the radical demands. An assessment of the adequacy of the reasons for accepting Christian participation in war and of the distinctions to accommodate the Sermon on the Mount is a task for a later study.

NOTES

1. Adolf Harnack, *Militia Christi: The Christian Religion and the Military in the First Three Centuries*, trans. by David McInnes Gracie (Philadelphia: Fortress Press, 1981), 100.

2. Ronald H. Bainton, *Christian Attitudes Toward War and Peace* (Nashville and New York: Abingdon Press, 1960), 68; John Helgeland, "Christians and the Roman Army A.D. 173-337," *Church History* 43 (1974): 149-63, 200.

3. Jean-Michel Hornus, *It Is Not Lawful for Me to Fight*, trans. by Alan Kreider and Oliver Coburn (Scottdale, Pa.: Herald Press, 1980).

4. See John the Baptist's statement "Rob no one by violence or by false accusation, and be content with your wages" (Luke 3:14).

5. Bainton, *Christian Attitudes*, 66 (italics added). There is considerable controversy about whether the church or at least some Christians drew a sharp distinction between the police functions of soldiers and their military function. Bainton (pp. 79-81) holds that the distinction is important, for example, to make sense of Canon III of the Synod of Arles (A.D. 314): "Concerning those, who throw down their arms in time of peace, we have decreed that they should be kept from communion." But critics contend that the "police work" interpretation is built on a false assumption: "that police duties were peaceful and that military duties were violent, or potentially so." Helgeland continues: "The distinction between civil and military preservation of order is largely a modern, not a Roman one. Acting in various capacities, the soldiers did most of the policing of the empire. Capturing terrorists, criminal investigation, finding missing persons, questioning suspects (torture), raiding houses in search of illegal weapons, collecting tariffs and tolls and spying were the duties which concerned many Roman soldiers acting as police" (Helgeland, "Christians and the Roman Army A.D. 173-337," 162-63).

6. Bainton, *Christian Attitudes*, chap. 5

7. Bernhard Schöpf, *Das Tötungsrecht bei den frühchristlichen Schriftstellern* (Regensburg: Friedrich Pustet, 1958).

8. For example, Gerard Caspary contends that "Origen's opposition to Christian participation in warfare is . . . quite openly based on the act of killing. There is not a word about the points so dear to anti-pacifist historians: nothing about the military oath, nothing about the pagan sacrifices soldiers supposedly had to perform." He also notes that "it is essentially because of [the] eschatological role" of Christians that they are "forbidden to fight in the Emperor's wars" (Gerard E. Caspary, *Politics and Exegesis: Origen and the Two Swords* [Berkeley and Los Angeles: University of California Press, 1979], 128, 126). For an analysis of Tertullian's emphasis on divided loyalty, see Stephen Gero, "Miles Gloriosus:

The Christian and Military Service according to Tertullian," *Church History* 39 (1970): 285–98. For more general discussions, see Bainton, *Christian Attitudes;* Hornus, *It Is Not Lawful for Me to Fight;* Peter Brock, *Pacifism in Europe to 1914* (Princeton: Princeton University Press); and Cecil John Cadoux, *The Early Christian Attitude to War* (New York: Seabury Press, 1982).

9. Hans von Campenhausen, "Christians and Military Service in the Early Church," *Tradition and Life in the Church: Essays and Lectures on Church History,* trans. by A. V. Littledale (Philadelphia: Fortress Press, 1968), 162–64.

10. William K. Frankena, *Ethics,* 2d ed. (Englewood Cliffs, N.J.: Prentice-Hall, 1973), 47.

11. Von Campenhausen, "Christians and Military Service in the Early Church," 167.

12. Brock, *Pacifism in Europe to 1914,* 14.

13. Frederick H. Russell, *The Just War in the Middle Ages* (Cambridge: Cambridge University Press, 1975), 17.

14. Ibid.

15. Ambrose, "On the Duties of the Clergy," in *Some of the Principal Works of St. Ambrose. A Select Library of Nicene and Post-Nicene Fathers,* 2d series, vol. X (New York: The Christian Literature Co., 1896), 30.

16. Ibid.

17. Marcus Tullius Cicero, *De Officiis,* trans. by Walter Miller, Loeb Classical Library (Cambridge: Harvard University Press, 1913), 1.7

18. In the contemporary context, pacifists set a limit on means at (a) or (b), whereas just warriors such as Paul Ramsey argue for a sharp line between (c) and (d). Both positions make the same theological-ethical appeals: we are not responsible for outcomes, for making history come out right, or for everything that happens, if prevention of evil (beneficence 2) would require immoral actions. Even though they draw the lines and set the limits at different places, they use this theological-ethical appeal to sustain respect for whatever line or limit has been accepted regarding the use of force. For further analysis, see James F. Childress, *Moral Responsibility in Conflicts: Essays on Nonviolence, War and Conscience* (Baton Rouge: Louisiana State University Press, 1982).

19. In an excellent discussion of negative responsibility, Bernard Williams writes: "It is because consequentialism attaches value ultimately to states of affairs, and its concern with what states of affairs the world contains, that it essentially involves the notion of *negative responsibility:* that if I am ever responsible for anything, then I must be just as much responsible for things that I allow or fail to prevent, as I am for things that I myself, in the more everyday restricted sense, bring about." ("A Critique of Utilitarianism," in J. J. C. Smart and Bernard Williams, *Utilitarianism: For and Against* [Cambridge: Cambridge University Press, 1973], 95).

20. Origen *Contra Celsum,* trans. with intro. and notes by Henry Chadwick (Cambridge: Cambridge University Press, 1953). All subsequent references to this volume will appear in parentheses in the text.

21. Von Campenhausen, "Christians and Military Service in the Early Church," 164.

22. Marcus George Singer, *Generalization in Ethics* (New York: Alfred A. Knopf, 1961), 4–5.

23. John Howard Yoder, *The Original Revolution: Essays on Christian Pacifism* (Scottdale, Pa.: Herald Press, 1971), 123. See also idem, *Nevertheless: The Varieties of Religious Pacifism* (Scottdale, Pa.: Herald Press, 1971), 73–77, 81–85.

24. Von Campenhausen, "Christians and Military Service in the Early Church," 166.

25. Harnack, *Militia Christi.*

26. Cecil John Cadoux, *The Early Church and the World* (Edinburgh: T. & T. Clark, 1925), 363. Stephen Gero notes that Tertullian's "statement that Christians do accept their fair share of the civic burdens appears also in Justin Martyr, and perhaps goes back to the commonplaces of Hellenistic Jewish apologetic," as in Philo, for example ("Miles Gloriosus," 293).

27. Von Campenhausen, "Christians and Military Service in the Early Church," 166.

28. Cadoux, *The Early Church and the World*, 412.

29. LeRoy Brandt Walters, Jr., "Five Classic Just-War Theories: A Study in the Thought of Thomas Aquinas, Vitoria, Suárez, Gentili, and Grotius" (Ph.D. dissertation, Yale University, 1971).

30. Cadoux, *The Early Church and the World*, 412; idem, *The Early Christian Attitude to War*, 15.

31. Hornus, *It Is Not Lawful for Me to Fight*, 188.

32. Bainton, *Christian Attitudes*, 84; Russell, *The Just War in the Middle Ages*, 12; and Cadoux, *The Early Church and the World*, 578.

33. Cadoux, *The Early Church and the World*, 469.

34. Ambrose, "On the Duties of the Clergy."

35. Reuven Kimelman, "Non-Violence in the Talmud," in *The Religious Situation: 1969*, ed. Donald R. Cutler (Boston: Beacon Press, 1969).

36. Ambrose, "On the Duties of the Clergy," 70–72.

37. Augustine, "Letters," *A Select Library of the Nicene and Post-Nicene Fathers of the Christian Church*, vol. 1 (New York: The Christian Literature Co., 1886), 47.5.

38. *The Political Writings of St. Augustine*, ed. by Henry Paolucci (Chicago: Henry Regnery Co., 1960), 150–51.

39. Ibid., 77, 182.

40. Russell, *The Just War in the Middle Ages*, 32 n. 63.

41. Quoted in Hornus, *It Is Not Lawful For Me to Fight*, 110.

42. Basil, "Letters," *St. Basil: Letters and Select Works, A Select Library of Nicene and Post-Nicene Fathers*, 2d series, vol. VIII (New York: The Christian Literature Co., 1895), 228; Bainton, *Christian Attitudes*, 78.

43. St. Augustine, "Reply to Faustus the Manichaean," *A Select Library of the Nicene and Post-Nicene Fathers of the Christian Church*, vol. IV (Buffalo: The Christian Literature Co., 1887), 22.70.

44. *The Political Writings of St. Augustine*, 165.

7

THE SIMPLE STRUCTURE
OF THE "JUST-WAR" THEORY

LEROY WALTERS

My aim in this essay is to present the simple structure that underlies the detailed discussions of war presented by several classic just-war theorists. The approach of the essay will be expository and analytical rather than critical. My hope is that persons who accept a contemporary version of the just-war theory will find the following description to be a sympathetic interpretation of the tradition which they have adapted as their own.

THE GENERAL FRAMEWORK

In his lecture "On the Law of War," first delivered about 1539, the sixteenth-century Spanish Dominican moral theologian Francisco de Vitoria (c. 1486–1546) presented a lively, compact synthesis of the theological and legal discussions of war which had been handed down to him. Vitoria's lecture treated "four principal questions":

- Whether it is lawful for Christians to wage war at all.
- Who has authority either to wage or to declare war?
- What can and ought to be causes of just war?
- What is lawful in a just war and how much may lawfully be done to the enemy?[1]

Vitoria's first question might be called the Pacifism Question. If killing and therefore the waging of war are always wrong—whether for Christians

---

LeRoy Walters is director of the Center for Bioethics, Kennedy Institute of Ethics, and associate professor of philosophy at Georgetown University. His Yale University Ph.D. dissertation was a historical study of the just-war tradition, entitled "Five Classic Just-War Theories: A Study in the Thought of Thomas Aquinas, Vitoria, Suárez, Gentili, and Grotius" (1971).

or for human beings in general—then the discussion of war and morality is at an end. On the other hand, if the waging of war can be morally legitimate in principle, then the theorist of just war is obliged to spell out the criteria of morally legitimate (or just) war. These criteria of just war are precisely the remaining three questions raised by Vitoria, which I will call the Authority Question, the Cause Question, and the Conduct Question. The Authority Question addressed the simple but important issue of official public sanction for the waging of war. The Cause Question considered what might be called legitimate or sufficient reasons for going to war. In subsequent international-law discussions this question has come to be known as the *jus ad bellum*, or the right to enter upon a war. When a war has begun, the Conduct Question, or the limits of permissible violence in war, becomes important. In international law this fourth question is called *jus in bello*, or justice in war.

Vitoria's four questions were adopted in slightly modified form by Francisco Suárez (1548–1617) and Hugo Grotius (1583–1645) in their later writings on the just war.[2] Since Vitoria, Suárez, and Grotius are generally considered three of the most important classic just-war theorists, one can safely conclude that the questions of Pacifism, Authority, Cause, and Conduct do constitute the general framework of the just-war theory. The next four sections of this essay briefly explain what topics the just-war theorists included in their discussions of the four questions. In the concluding section I explore the logical relationships among the four questions.

THE PACIFISM QUESTION

The just-war theorists were keenly aware of tensions between the waging of war and the ethical teachings of the New Testament. Particularly troublesome passages were the Sermon on the Mount, Jesus' statement that those who take the sword will perish by the sword, Jesus' rebuke of Peter for having defended Jesus with the sword, and St. Paul's discussions of love and nonresistance (Matt. 5:38–48; 26:52; John 18:11; Romans 13). The major theorists also acknowledged the presence of a pacifist tradition within the Christian church, a tradition that seemed to begin with Tertullian and Origen and to continue with Wycliffe, Erasmus, and the Anabaptists.

The just-war theorists employed a three-pronged strategy in their response to the pacifist tradition. First, they fused elements of Stoic philosophy, the Roman law, and the Old Testament into a notion of the law of nature which permitted the waging of war. Perhaps the most basic text was the Roman law's assertion that "force may be repelled by force."[3] The law

136

of nature was further elucidated by Abraham's wars against four kings,[4] and Cicero's writings, especially *On Duties*. The theorists went on to assert that "the Gospel law forbids nothing which is allowed by natural law."[5]

Given this assumption about the harmony of the law of nature and the gospel, a way had to be found to limit the scope of application of pacifist-like New Testament texts. Augustine had undertaken this task in the fourth century. The nonresistant texts, he argued, were directed toward private transactions among individuals and toward the "preparation of the mind" rather than toward external actions by legitimate political authorities. Augustine's views, mediated by the medieval canon law, were adopted virtually without change by the major just-war theorists. This mode of interpreting New Testament Scripture constituted the second prong in the theorists' response to pacifism.

The third major mode of argument employed by just-war theorists on the Pacifism Question was an appeal to tradition—"the authority and example of good and holy men."[6] Constantine the Great, Theodosius the Great, and other Christian emperors waged many wars, Vitoria noted, despite the fact that their councils included "bishops of great sanctity and learning."[7] The pacifist objections of Tertullian and Origen were viewed as context-dependent reservations about idolatrous demands by contemporary Roman armies, and their authority was thought to be more than counterbalanced by the combined weight of Augustine, canon law, and the practice of the church.

THE AUTHORITY QUESTION

If war was in principle morally justified, there remained the task of specifying the conditions under which the *waging* of war was actually justified. One obvious problem to be addressed was: by whom may war be declared or waged? I have called this problem the Authority Question.

On one central point all the just-war theorists were unanimous: the prince has authority to wage war. Beginning with Thomas Aquinas, the tradition employed Aristotle's notion of the state (or republic) as a perfect community, sufficient to itself and competent not only to defend itself but also to punish wrongdoers. In short, the just-war theorists developed a doctrine of sovereignty and proclaimed that the power to wage war was an important aspect of the sovereign's authority.

The theorists generally condemned private wars, arguing that private citizens could appeal to a higher authority for redress. The right of personal self-defense at the time of attack, however, was accorded to private individuals by all just-war theorists after Augustine. What was reserved to the state was the authority to use force either after an attack had ceased—"after an interval" was the technical phrase—or as a means of punishment.

There were, as one would expect, debates among the just-war theorists about precisely which rulers had authority to wage war. For example, Vitoria assumed that the Republic of Venice and the Kingdom of Castile and Aragon were perfect communities but argued that the duke of Alva and the count of Benevento did not possess war-making authority except in extraordinary circumstances.[8] More significantly, Grotius and some of the Spanish authors disagreed on the political status of the Low Countries: Grotius asserted their independence while Balthasar Ayala condemned their leaders as rebels against the legitimate authority of the king of Spain.[9] However, the theorists' general answer to the Authority Question and their rationale for that answer were clear.

The just-war tradition's insistence on princely authority did not exclude the possibility of just revolution. Revolution—or resistance to a tyrannous ruler, as the medieval and early modern writers would have phrased it—was explicitly advocated by all the just-war theorists, at least in extreme circumstances. Resistance to tyranny, however, was viewed as occurring within a perfect community; thus revolution was precisely not war.

It is easy to modernize the Authority Question by focusing attention only on the role of the secular state. However, several of the classic just-war theorists also regarded the church as an appropriate authority for declaring war in cases where the Christian faith was threatened. Aquinas accepted without question the church's role in launching the Crusades to recover the holy land from unbelievers.[10] In a similar vein, Vitoria and Suárez argued that the pope could declare war and call together Christian believers if the faith were threatened by infidel (presumably Moslem) attack or if Christian missionary activity were obstructed by unbelievers.[11] For understandable reasons Protestant just-war theorists, like Giovanni Gentili and Grotius, were skeptical of the pope's war-making authority. Grotius did propose a functional equivalent, however, namely, "that all Christians are under obligation to enter a league against the enemies of Christianity."[12] In twentieth-century discussions of just war, the Authority Question is of course confined to the secular state.

THE CAUSE QUESTION

The central issue discussed by the classic just-war theorists was the Cause Question. Indeed, it is probably because of the notion of just cause that the predominant Western theory about war and morality is called the *just*-war theory.

The notion of cause employed by the theorists was not that of a sequence of events each producing another event. In other words, the theorists were not asking, "What events resulted in a war?" Rather, their usage was akin to our usage when we, considering whether to file a lawsuit or not, ask an attorney, "Do I have a cause of action?" A cause in this sense is a good reason or a rationale for some kind of counteraction in response to an offense by a second party.

The offense by the second party will not be just any immoral act, for example, a failure to act charitably; rather, the other party's offense had to violate the natural order of justice. In fact, in the Latin which Christian just-war theorists from Augustine to Grotius employed in their writings the usual word for an offense that was a just cause for war was *injuria*—a term that meant both injury and injustice. Thus, *just* wars were precisely those which were waged for the *just* cause of resisting or avenging *injustice*.

There were three widely accepted just causes of war: defense, recovery of property, and punishment. Wars waged for the first cause were always defensive. Wars waged to punish were always offensive in the sense that the enemy was not at the moment on one's territory. Wars to recover property could be either defensive or offensive, depending on the circumstances.

Assuming that a state's boundaries were not in dispute and that the title of the ruler and citizens to their property was clear, the notion of a defensive war was quite obvious. An enemy force crossed one's boundary and began seizing the property of one's citizens. In this situation the ruler and the citizens of the invaded state had the right to defend themselves, to repossess their property if possible, and to push the invader back to the original boundary. This right of states and their rulers was viewed as analogous to the private citizen's right to repel force by force and was considered so obvious that the classic just-war theorists expended relatively little time discussing it.[13] If ever the notion of necessity applied, it was in the case of actual invasion by an enemy force.

Much more central to the classic theorists' discussions were offensive wars undertaken for the purpose of avenging injustice and punishing the perpetrators of injustice. Here the relevant analogy was not personal self-defense but rather the state's domestic role in punishing its own citizens for crimes they have committed. Thus, an appropriate model for wars of punishment would be sanctions applied to an offending state by an international police force sponsored by an international agency (like the United Nations). The theorists realized that no such international force existed but argued that a prince acting justly could fulfill the same disinterested role.

The notions of last resort, proportionality, and reasonable hope of success were applied by the theorists almost exclusively to offensive war. Last resort meant that peaceful means for rectifying the injustice should be explored before a punitive war was undertaken. Proportionality meant simply that the punishment should fit the enemy's crime. Just as execution was an excessive punishment for petty theft on the domestic scene, so war was an inappropriate means for punishing slight international offenses. In Vitoria's words,

> Not every kind and degree of injustice suffices for commencing a war. The proof of this is that even with one's own fellow-countrymen it is not permitted for every offense to impose atrocious punishments, like death or exile or confiscation of goods. Since, then, the things which occur in war are all serious and atrocious—such as deaths, fires, and devastations—it is not permitted for slight injustices to pursue the authors of the injustices, since the degree of punishment ought to be in close correspondence to the offense (Deuteronomy 25).[14]

The reasonable-hope-of-success notion also applied chiefly if not exclusively to offensive wars waged to punish injustice. The obvious point of this requirement was that if one sought to punish injustice by means of war but lost the war, the result might be an even more unjust outcome. For Suárez a fifty-fifty chance of success in a punitive war was sufficient.[15] Grotius was somewhat more stringent, however, arguing that "as in the case of a civil judge, he who wishes to avenge crimes by armed force ought to be much more powerful than the other party."[16]

In addition to discussing general causes of war and rules for deciding when to undertake an offensive war, the classic just-war theorists identified specific reasons for going to war. These specific reasons make it clear that the Cause Question was directed chiefly against two kinds of opponents. On the political level, the theorists denied that mere reasons of state constituted a sufficient cause for war. In Vitoria's words,

> Extension of empire is not a just cause of war.

> Neither the personal glory of the prince nor any other advantage to him is a just cause of war.[17]

While Vitoria, Suárez, and Grotius did not mention Machiavelli by name, they were clearly aware of his views and flatly contradicted his power-politics model, affirming instead a model in which all states were obliged to adhere to a supranational standard of justice.

At the religious level, the major sixteenth- and seventeenth-century theorists were at pains to deny that the mere acceptance of non-Christian beliefs by Moslems or Native Americans in the New World was a sufficient ground for war. In this emphasis they followed Aquinas's clear assertion of religious liberty, unless and until unbelievers committed injustice against

Christians or innocent unbelievers, for example, the victims of human sacrifice.

Despite their agreement on the general just causes for war and on several specific reasons for going to war, the classic just-war theorists diverged in their views on other specific grounds for waging war. At the natural level, Vitoria and Suárez opposed, while Grotius condoned, wars waged to punish sexual practices thought to be opposed to the law of nature, for example, homosexuality and bestiality.[18] On the other hand, Vitoria and Suárez regarded injury to the reputation or honor of a prince or state as a sufficient reason for war, while Grotius probably did not.[19] At the supernatural level, Suárez viewed heresy as a sufficient cause for war in some circumstances, while the Protestant Grotius, adherent of a faith which Suárez would have regarded as heretical, did not. Vitoria and Suárez argued against waging war merely because the offending people were idolatrous, but Grotius argued that war could be justified if the idols were morally evil.[20]

The theorists' disagreements about specific reasons for war suggest the possibility that two different theorists might view the same action by a second party and disagree about whether that action constituted a sufficient reason for war. The theorists themselves did not discuss this potential problem in answering the Cause Question. They did, however, explicitly treat an analogous problem, namely, that two different parties—for example, two hostile princes—might perceive or describe a factual situation differently and consequently might each conclude that a just cause for war against the other existed. Vitoria, Suárez, and Grotius all envisaged such a contingency and all responded to the question, "Can a war simultaneously be just on both sides?"

Given the classic theorists' acceptance of an objective, supranational standard of justice, one would not expect them to have admitted that a war could be just for both contending parties. Victoria, Suárez, and Grotius were sensitive to the possibility of moral error even by conscientious persons, however, and all accepted the notion that a war could be objectively just on one side and subjectively just on the other. That is, the prince and soldiers waging an unjust war could be sincerely, unavoidably mistaken, and thus subjectively innocent, while doing objectively unjust acts. In Vitoria's words,

> It is not incongruous to assert that there is a just war on both sides when on the one side there is right *(jus)* and on the other invincible ignorance.[21]

Thus far we have considered only the role of rulers in judging whether the cause of a war was just. There remains the question of the role of ordinary soldiers or citizens in assessing the justice of a cause—a problem that in the twentieth century has come to be called the issue of selective conscientious objection. In general, the classic just-war theorists held princes and kings to a more stringent standard of responsibility for judging the cause of war. Vitoria and Suárez argued that the ordinary citizen was under no moral obligation to examine whether the cause of a war was just and that in cases of doubt the citizen's presumptive duty to obey the prince took precedence over the doubt. In Vitoria's words,

> If subjects in a case of doubt do not follow their prince to war, they expose themselves to the risk of betraying their State to the enemy, and this is a much more serious thing than fighting against the enemy despite a doubt. [22]

Grotius, however, expressed strong sympathy for a minority view in the just-war tradition, namely, that in cases of doubt a subject ought not to serve in a war, even at the command of his or her prince. In Grotius's view, Vitoria's discussion of the morally safer course had described the moral options involved incorrectly. According to Grotius,

> Disobedience in things of this kind, by its very nature, is a lesser evil than manslaughter, especially than the slaughter of many innocent men. [23]

Despite their apparent disagreement in doubtful cases, Vitoria, Suárez, and Grotius were unanimous in their view that a boundary case could occur and that the injustice of one's national cause could be evident; in that case, the logic of the just-war theory obliged them to advocate selective conscientious objection. Vitoria formulated this moral rule as follows:

> The proofs and tokens of the injustice of war may be such that ignorance would be no excuse even to the subjects who serve in it. This is clear because such ignorance (on the part of subjects) might be deliberate and adopted with evil intent toward the enemy. [24]

To clinch his point, Vitoria cited three examples that would undoubtedly have impressed his readers. If subjects were not held responsible for participating in the injustice of their leaders, he argued, then

> unbelievers would be excused when they follow their leader to war against Christians. . . . Also, the solders who crucified Christ, ignorantly following Pilate's order, would be excused. In addition, the Jewish mob would be excused which was led by the elders to shout, "Away with Him, crucify Him." [25]

THE CONDUCT QUESTION

Even in cases when a war is begun for a just cause—the issue of *jus ad bellum*—there remains the question of just conduct in the war *(jus in bello)*.

Grotius introduced his discussion of the Conduct Question with the following words:

> We have considered who may wage war and for what causes it is lawful to fight. It follows that we should consider what is lawful in war and how much and by what means *(modis)*. [26]

In analyzing the Conduct Question, the classic just-war theorists continued to employ the familiar metaphors of personal self-defense, recapture of stolen property, and judicial action in punishing offenders. The right of the state to ward off invaders and to recapture property taken from the state or its citizens received little attention in the writings of the theorists because such conduct in war seemed so obviously just. [27] What was of much more interest to the sixteenth- and seventeenth-century theorists was the extent to which the ruler of an aggrieved state could assess damages against the offending state (a civil-law analogy) and punish the ruler or citizens of the offending state (a criminal-law analogy). Both actions would normally have involved offensive war in the sense that the aggrieved state would usually have had to carry the battle across the original state boundary into the enemy's territory in order to extract the appropriate amount of damages or to inflict the appropriate punishment on the original perpetrators of the injustice. [28]

The magnitude of the enemy's offense determined the extent to which the ruler of the aggrieved state could retaliate in a just war. In other words, a relationship of proportionality between the severity of the enemy's offense and the amount of damages and punishment was to be achieved, and the ruler of the aggrieved state was asked to act as justly in the international sphere as a judge awarding damages or imposing a sentence in the domestic sphere. [29]

The Conduct Question was divided into two parts, appropriate conduct during active hostilities and appropriate conduct after the conclusion of the war. During the phase of active hostilities, the general rule adopted unanimously by Vitoria, Suárez, Grotius, and their contemporaries was the following: If the cause of a war is just (and the war is therefore a just war), *all necessary means* may be employed to win the war and thereby to promote justice. Suárez formulated this rule in the following words:

> If the end is lawful, the necessary means are also lawful. And hence, in the whole course and duration of a war, virtually nothing can be done which contains injustice, except the [deliberate] killing of innocent persons. For all other damages are ordinarily judged necessary for attaining the end of war. [30]

Harm to innocent persons during the conduct of a just war was, of course, a matter of major concern to the classic theorists, since the injury or killing of an innocent person was, by definition, unjust. All the theorists urged that collateral damage to civilians during war be limited to the minimum amount required to win the war. Yet, in cases of necessity, the theorists permitted the storming or assaulting of a city,[31] the bombarding of a ship or a house full of thieves even if "a few infants, women or other innocent persons" were exposed to possible harm,[32] and even the sack of a city[33]—if such action was necessary for victory in a just war. Vitoria justified the sack of a city with the following argument:

> Is it lawful to permit soldiers to sack a city? I answer . . . : This is not unlawful in itself *(per se)* if it is necessary for the waging of war or as a deterrent to the enemy or to kindle the spirits of the soldiers. . . . This action is lawful on the same ground as the burning of a city for a reasonable cause. Nevertheless, such permission to sack results in many horrors and cruelties, which are committed beyond all humane limits by barbarous soldiers: the slaughter and torture of the innocent, the rape of virgins, the violation of married women, and the looting of temples; it is therefore extremely iniquitous to give over a city, especially a Christian city, to sack without the greatest necessity and weightiest reason. *But if the necessity of war requires such action, it is not unlawful,* even if it is probable that the soldiers will perpetrate foul misdeeds of this kind, which their leaders are nevertheless bound to forbid and, as far as possible, to prevent.[34]

In contrast, Grotius regarded the pillaging of a city as almost invariably a disproportionate means of warfare.

> Such actions cannot take place without very serious harm to many innocent persons, and often are of little consequence for the result of the war; so that Christian goodness almost always, and bare justice very often, shrinks from them.[35]

After the conclusion of hostilities, the second and more precise phase in the assessment and recovery of damages and the punishment of offenders began. In this process the ruler who had successfully waged a just war again functioned in the role of judge. In the postwar Nuremberg-like judicial proceedings, damages were assessed through the seizure of enemy property and through the enslavement of prisoners of war. Innocent persons could not be despoiled or enslaved unless the full measure of compensatory and punitive damages could not otherwise be collected.[36] Similarly, the ruler of the forces that had victoriously waged a just war meted out punishment to guilty enemy persons. The precise identity of the guilty was a matter of dispute among the sixteenth- and seventeenth-century just-war theorists. Suárez regarded all enemy combatants as guilty.[37] Vitoria, on the other hand, attributed personal guilt to Moslem soldiers who had participated in war against Christians but tended to exonerate both Christian and Native American warriors.[38] In the opinion of Grotius, the stigma of guilt attached only to soldiers who had engaged in an unjust war both consciously and voluntarily.[39]

The punishment normally prescribed for the guilty was either execution or enslavement. Guided by Old Testament precedents, Vitoria and Suárez advocated the liberal application of the death penalty in certain cases. In Vitoria's view all guilty Moslem soldiers could legitimately be slain if such a measure was necessary to ensure future "peace and security."[40] While conceding that the postwar "slaying of a great multitude of guilty persons" was a measure to be employed "only when there was most urgent cause," Suárez argued that "even such slaughter may sometimes be allowed, in order to terrify the rest."[41] Grotius, however, urged moderation in the postwar employment of the death penalty, asserting that the crime of the guilty enemy soldier must have been of sufficient magnitude to justify the sentence of capital punishment by a domestic criminal court; even such vicious criminals should be pardoned, Grotius urged, "if their number is very great."[42] Enslavement of the guilty was also employed as a postwar punishment, at least in wars between Christians and Moslems.[43]

From a theoretical standpoint, one can raise the question whether excessive injustice in the conduct of war, either during or after hostilities, could somehow vitiate the justice of one's cause and therefore raise a question about the justice of the war itself. The most explicit answer to this question was provided by Grotius: unjust conduct cannot render a just war unjust.

> Since an enemy, although waging a just war, does not have the true and perfect right of killing innocent subjects, who are not responsible for the war, unless either as a necessary defensive measure or as a result and apart from his purpose . . . , it follows that, if it is certain that the enemy comes with such a spirit that he absolutely refuses to spare the lives of hostile subjects when he can, these subjects may defend themselves by the law of nature, of which they are not deprived by the law of nations.
>
> But even then we shall not say that the *war* is just on both sides; for it is not a question of the *war*, but of a certain and definite *act*. This *act*, moreover, although done by him who in other respects has a right to wage war, *is unjust*, and hence is justly resisted.[44]

The apparent stringency of the just-war theorists' answer to the Conduct Question is based in part on the judicial model which the theory presupposed. The rules for proper conduct in war applied to one side only—the side involved in the enforcement of the natural law or the side having a just cause. Military counteraction by the other side was viewed as akin to contempt of court or resisting arrest. A twentieth-century interpreter of Grotius captured the spirit of this judicial model in the following words:

> The rules of warfare in Grotius' book are rules for such states (nations) only as wage a just war against either wrong *(inuria)* or crime *(maleficium)*, rules for a *bellum justum* or *bellum pium*. They are neither, therefore, intended for the culprit state, nor for two states who are equally wrongdoers.[45]

THE RELATIONSHIP AMONG THE QUESTIONS

The relationship among the Pacifism Question, the Authority Question, and the Conduct Question can be analyzed from at least two perspectives. The first is that of Thomistic ethics. In his detailed treatment of ethical theory Thomas Aquinas distinguished three primary aspects of a moral act: (1) the object or objective *(objectum)* of the act, (2) the circumstances *(circumstantiae)* of the act, and (3) the end *(finis)* of the act.[46] He argued that a defect with respect to any of these aspects made an act immoral, but not necessarily unjust, since injustice is but one of several types of immorality.[47]

According to Aquinas's theory, the object of an act specified the kind of act that was contemplated, for example, theft, adultery, or war. Some objects he regarded as intrinsically evil; others were indifferent. The circumstances of an act concerned the questions who, what, where, by what means, why, in what manner, and when.[48] Sometimes, in Aquinas's view, the circumstances of an act had an important bearing on its morality, although they did not necessarily do so. In contrast, the end of an act referred to the agent's goal, purpose, or intention in performing the act.[49]

Aquinas and the later just-war theorists discussed the Pacifism Question in order to assert that war, unlike theft, is not an intrinsically evil act. Thus, the way was clear to discuss the proper circumstances and the proper end of war. The Authority Question responded to the who-circumstance, the Cause Question to the why-circumstance, and the Conduct Question to the in-what-manner-circumstance. If all of these circumstances were appropriate, there remained the question of the agent's intention in waging war. In Aquinas, the right intention of warriors was one of three major criteria of just war. By the time of these sixteenth- and seventeenth-century theorists the notion of intention was only vestigially present; however, these later theorists did continue to assert that the goal and aim of war was to be peace. Thus, war could be a moral act, proper in its object, its circumstances, and its end.

There existed special links between morally permissible war and the principle of justice. War was to be initiated by the prince or king, whose primary role was to preserve justice and to punish wrongdoers both within and outside of the realm. The war itself was just if it had a just cause. The conduct of the war was just if the response to the aggrieved party was proportionate to the offense against it and if both the war and the postwar judicial proceeding were directed against the perpetrators of injustice. Individual acts of injustice in the conduct of war might require restitution, but they were not thought to vitiate the justice of the cause or of the war as a whole.[50]

A second perspective from which to view the interrelationship of the four major questions of the just-war theory is the twentieth-century terminology of necessary and sufficient conditions. On this view, the answer to the Pacifism Question is that war can be just if certain conditions are fulfilled. These conditions are then specified by the Authority Question and the Cause Question, which indicate the two conditions that are individually necessary and jointly sufficient for a just *war*. The Conduct Question can only be raised when the prior three questions have been satisfactorily answered. This final question does not specify a necessary condition for just war. Rather, it directs our attention to the necessary and sufficient conditions of just conduct in a just war.

NOTES

1. Francisco de Vitoria *De jure belli*, prologue (author's translation).
2. Francisco Suárez *De bello* 1.7; Hugo Grotius *De jure belli ac pacis*, prologue, 33–35; 1.2; 3.1, title and first paragraph.
3. *Digest* 1.1.3.
4. Genesis 14.
5. Vitoria *De jure belli* 1. Unless otherwise noted, this and all subsequent quotations from Vitoria, Suárez, and Grotius are taken from the Classics of International Law translations of their works.
6. Ibid.
7. Ibid.
8. Ibid., 7–9.
9. Hugo Grotius *De jure praedae* 11 (pp. 169–70); cf. 13 (pp. 283–89); Balthasar Ayala *De jure et officiis bellicis* 1.2, 17.
10. Thomas Aquinas *Summa theologiae* II–II, 188, 3, ad 3; *Quodlibetum* 2.16.
11. Francisco de Vitoria *De potestate civili* 1.5.13; Suárez *De bello* 5.7; *De fide*, disp. 18.1, 4, 7.
12. Grotius *De jure belli ac pacis* 2.15.12, title.
13. Ibid., 2.1.3–18.
14. Vitoria *De jure belli* 14 (author's translation).
15. Suárez *De bello* 4.10.

16. Grotius *De jure belli ac pacis* 2.24.7.
17. Vitoria *De jure belli* 11 and 12.
18. LeRoy Brandt Walters, Jr., "Five Classic Just-War Theories: A Study in the Thought of Thomas Aquinas, Vitoria, Suárez, Gentili, and Grotius" (Ph.D. diss., Yale University, 1971), 340–41, 346–47.
19. Ibid., 340–41.
20. Ibid., 346–47.
21. Francisco de Vitoria *De Indis* 3.6 (author's translation).
22. Vitoria *De jure belli* 31.
23. Grotius *De jure belli ac pacis* 2.26.4, 5.
24. Vitoria *De jure belli* 26.
25. Ibid. (Classics of International Law translation, slightly revised).
26. Grotius *De jure belli ac pacis* 3.1.1 (author's translation).
27. Vitoria *De jure belli* 15 and 16.
28. Ibid., 17–19.
29. Ibid.
30. Suárez *De bello* 7.6.
31. Vitoria *De jure belli* 37.
32. Grotius *De jure belli ac pacis* 3.1.4.1.
33. Vitoria *De jure belli* 52.
34. Ibid. (author's translation and italics).
35. Grotius *De jure belli ac pacis* 3.12.8.4.
36. Vitoria *De jure belli* 42; Suárez *De bello* 7.12; Grotius *De jure belli ac pacis* 3.14.1–2.
37. Suárez *De bello* 7.16.
38. Vitoria *De jure belli* 48.
39. Grotius *De jure belli ac pacis* 3.11.3–6.
40. Vitoria *De jure belli* 48.
41. Suárez *De bello* 7.7. In their discussion of this issue, the basic Old Testament text for both Suárez and Vitoria was Deuteronomy 20, esp. vv. 13–14.
42. Grotius *De jure belli ac pacis* 3.11.16.1; 3.11.17, title.
43. Vitoria *De jure belli* 42; Suárez *De bello* 7.13; Grotius *De jure belli ac pacis* 3.7.9; 3.14.9; 3.21.23–30.
44. Grotius *De jure belli ac pacis* 3.26.6.1, 2 (italics added).
45. C. Val Vollenhoven, *Framework of Grotius' Book De Iure Belli ac Pacis* (Amsterdam: N. V. Noord-Hollandsche Uitgeversmaatschappij, 1931), 89.
46. Aquinas *Summa theologiae* 1–2.18.2–4.
47. Ibid., 18.4, ad 3; 19.6, ad 1.
48. Ibid., 7.3.
49. Ibid., 20.2; cf. 18.6; 19.7.
50. Grotius *De jure belli ac pacis* 3.26.6.1, 2.

III

TWO CURRENT
PUBLIC CONCERNS

8

OBJECTION TO PARTICIPATION IN COMBAT: LEGALITY AND MORALITY

CHARLES P. LUTZ

Conscientious objection to combatant military service has been known from the beginning of United States history. In fact, legal exemption from military duty for objectors first appeared in colonial times, over one hundred years before the U.S. was founded. In 1661 Massachusetts set a precedent by relieving pacifists of military obligation. Rhode Island followed in 1673 and Pennsylvania in 1757.

This chapter will trace the development of conscientious objection in U.S. society and its evolution in U.S. law. It will discuss the dilemma of the selective objector and the social-policy ironies resulting from that position. Finally, it will look at the challenges posed for U.S. religious communities by the war/conscience tension.

CONSCIENTIOUS OBJECTION: U.S. HISTORY AND LAW

The Revolutionary War which gave birth to the nation also divided Americans. Historians estimate that as much as one-half of the population was either sympathetic with England or neutral. There were also proindependence people, like many of the Quakers and other pacifists, who simply did not accept violent means of achieving independence. The only effective conscripting into armed service during the Revolution was done by the colonies, not the Continental Congress. The colonies usually accommodated objectors by excusing them if they hired a substitute or paid a fee. Some of the colonies also allowed for noncombatant service in the military.

Charles P. Lutz is director of the Office of Church in Society, The American Lutheran Church.

As early as 1775 the Continental Congress enunciated the principle this nation still basically follows: "There are some people who from Religious Principles cannot bear Arms in any case," the delegates said, adding that they "intend no violence to their Consciences." The Congress then urged such persons to "contribute liberally, in this time of universal calamity, to the relief of their distressed brethren in the several colonies, and to do all other services to their oppressed country, which they can consistently with their Religious Principles."

Conscription was first proposed on a national basis in 1790, then again in 1814. Both attempts to introduce it were stopped with the argument that it is contrary to the spirit of liberty. Even the unpopular Mexican War was conducted without drafting men into uniform. The first conscription laws were enacted early in the Civil War. Both North and South passed legislation in 1862 allowing a draft of manpower. The North amended its law in 1863 to permit draftees to pay $300 in lieu of serving—thus establishing the American pattern of letting the draft fall more heavily on the poor. The most dramatic result was a three-day antidraft riot in New York City, which still stands as the bloodiest civil disturbance in our history: twelve hundred dead.

No regular provision was made for conscientious objectors until 1864, after peace church leaders had petitioned President Lincoln and the Congress. That provision called for objectors to perform various forms of alternate service. When some religious pacifists also refused alternate service, they were exempted from duty of any kind. There is also evidence that some men who qualified as conscientious objectors were forced into the armed forces and abused when they subsequently refused to fight. The idea of conscientious objection as a legal and moral act was not yet established.

The South also exempted peace church members for a time. But its law required the objector to provide a substitute who would serve or to pay a fee of $500. As the war progressed and the South became more desperate for manpower, this exemption was dropped. The CO in the South suffered doubly, for in almost every case he not only refused to bear arms but wanted to abolish slavery as well. The number of objectors during the Civil War was not impressive. Estimates are that less than fifteen hundred were registered as COs while there were two million men in uniform. But the significance of the precedent these men set cannot be overestimated.

Conscription did not return until 1917. The emotionalism and near-hysteria which surrounded our participation in World War I did not provide a congenial atmosphere for the conscientious objector. COs appeared in fairly large numbers (the term came into general usage during this war), but the draft law made no provision for them. Those who sought noncombatant service were usually given it by the military. But those who refused to enter military service were sent to federal prisons. Seventeen were sentenced to death. None of the sentences was carried out, but it was not until 1933 that President Roosevelt issued pardons releasing the last WWI objectors from prison.

Imprisoned COs in World War I totaled about five hundred, though it was estimated that another three hundred thousand draft avoiders were never prosecuted. Even the religious objectors were not recognized legally until near the end of the war. They were then excused if they would do unpaid work in agriculture or with the Red Cross.

After 1918 conscription again lapsed. It was not revived until the fall of 1940, when fear of the war in Europe led Congress to pass the first peacetime draft in America's history. The draft was highly unpopular in those days prior to our entry into World War II. When it came up for extension in August of 1941, it passed the crucial vote in Congress by one vote. After Pearl Harbor and our entry into the war, general resistance to conscription subsided, and the legislation was broadened. Except for two brief periods (nine months in 1947–48 and three months in 1971) conscription continued until 1973.

GENERAL CONSCIENTIOUS OBJECTION

The current basic provision for exemption of conscientious objectors was written into the 1940 Selective Training and Service Act. There were significant changes in 1948 and again with the major buildup of U.S. forces in Vietnam, 1965 and after. The 1940 law said exemption from military service (or a noncombatant role in service) would be granted to any man "who, by reason of religious training and belief, is conscientiously opposed to participation in war in any form." Membership in one of the traditional peace churches was not a prerequisite in the law, but in practice it continued to be easier for peace church members to gain the CO classification than for others.

In 1948 the draft law was amended by addition of the "Supreme Being" clause. It defined "religious training and belief" as "belief in a relation to a Supreme Being involving duties superior to those arising from any human relation. . . ." The task of interpreting the notion of a Supreme Being proved difficult. Was only the Christian (or Judeo-Christian) God recognized? Could a Supreme Being be a concept of some guiding force in the universe? Could someone with no religious affiliation be recognized as believing in a Supreme Being?

The issue finally came before the Supreme Court. In March of 1965, the Court made the following ruling in its Seeger decision:

> The test of belief "in a relation to a Supreme Being" is whether a given belief that is sincere and meaningful occupies a place in the life of its possessor parallel to that filled by the orthodox belief in God of one who clearly qualifies for exemption. Where such beliefs have parallel positions in the lives of their respective holders we cannot say that one is "in a relation to a Supreme Being" and the other is not.

The decision was important, since it expanded the definition of "religious training and belief" to include views not traditionally considered religious. But Congress, when it renewed the draft law in 1967, sought to narrow the Court's expanded interpretation. It dropped the Supreme Being clause and included only a negative definition of "religious training and belief" as not including "essentially political, sociological or philosophical views, or a merely personal moral code."

Again, the Supreme Court responded by throwing out that attempt to narrow the CO definition. The case involved a registrant, Elliott Welsh II, whose CO claim was rejected. Welsh had crossed out the word "religious" on his Selective Service form and had described his views as formed by readings in sociology and history. The Court held that persons for whom ethical and philosophical considerations are of prime importance should not be excluded from the CO provision. Nor should it exclude those who strongly oppose the nation's public policy, said the Court.

The new standard laid down by the Court in Welsh included "all those whose consciences, spurred by deeply held moral, ethical, or religious beliefs, would give them no rest or peace if they allowed themselves to become a part of an instrument of war." *The New York Times* commented editorially that the nation had at last abandoned the "implication that only those who subscribe to formal religions are to be credited with a fundamental aversion to war and killing."

The Welsh decision is thus far the high-water mark in the broadening of the CO provision under U.S. law. An attempt to open up the provision to objectors to particular wars was rejected by the Court in its Gillette decision (March 1971) by an 8-to-1 decision. The Court ruled that the Selective Service law did not allow selective objection. In late spring of 1971, an attempt to amend the draft law to legalize objection to particular wars was made in the Senate. Senator Philip Hart of Michigan sponsored the amendment, but only twelve votes were recorded in favor. The House did not consider such an amendment.

What is required for recognition as a conscientious objector under the present draft law? A claimant must persuade the local draft board that he qualifies under three considerations (that the law applies only to males was reaffirmed by the Supreme Court in 1981):

1. *He objects to "participation in war in any form."* He need not be opposed to all forms of violence—only the kind represented by war. But he must be able to show that his objection is to bearing arms in *any* war, and not just to a particular military situation.

2. *His objection arises from a central conviction.* The law does not require formal religious belief, but it does require evidence that the CO position is based on centrally held values, part of a pattern of belief or world view.

3. *He is sincere.* Proving sincerity is often the most difficult part of a CO claim, since it cannot really be proved but depends on how a draft board feels about the claim and the claimant.

Under the draft law as it operated during the Vietnam War, persons granted a CO claim were allowed to choose between noncombatant service within the military and civilian alternate service. The latter required the person "to perform two years of civilian work contributing to the maintenance of the national health, safety, and interest."

There is also provision for men who become conscientious objectors *after* entering the armed forces. All branches of service provide for the processing of requests for discharge or reassignment to noncombatant duties because of conscientious objection.

Selective Conscientious Objection

The increasing concern about conscience and war in past decades led many Americans to rediscover the morality of war was an issue in their religious traditions. Especially for Roman Catholics and most Protestants, and also to a degree for Jews, the "just-war ethic" was at the heart of their teaching. The theory was developed by Augustine, drawing upon the biblical tradition of both the Old and New Testaments. Thomas Aquinas in the thirteenth century elaborated the concept. The teaching was carried into mainstream Protestant theology by reformers such as Martin Luther and John Calvin.

The just-war teaching assumes that some wars can be justified from a moral perspective, and some clearly cannot be considered justifiable. The teaching tries to provide guidelines that will help answer the question: Is the particular war we are contemplating (or are already conducting) a justifiable war? The teaching was intended originally to assist rulers who had to decide about taking their people into war. It was not primarily intended as help to citizens for deciding whether they would follow their leaders. Until relatively recent times, it was more or less assumed that citizens would do what their leaders required, especially in the realm of foreign policy. But today the just-war ethic functions primarily as a guide for individuals who are faced with a decision about participating or not participating in a military activity.

One way of summarizing the just-war teaching is by listing seven tests for a war to be justifiable. The first four are considerations prior to embarking upon warfare. The final three are considerations related to the conduct of the warfare.

1. *Last resort.* The war can be entered only after *all* other means have been exhausted. All peaceful forms of negotiation must be attempted, and conceivably such tactics as a Gandhi-style campaign of nonviolent resistance should also be tried if applicable.

2. *Just cause.* One can justify engaging in war for reasons of self-defense, to protect the innocent from attack or to restore rights wrongfully denied, and to reestablish the order necessary for decent human existence.

3. *Declaration by lawful authority.* The war must be openly and legally declared by a properly constituted government, and its aims must be made known to the world. Such a declaration tells a potential enemy the conditions upon which a settlement could be made and war avoided. It also lets other nations assess the justice of the cause and set their own conduct accordingly.

4. *Prospect of success.* There must be a reasonable prospect of victory. National suicide and struggles in which annihilation of both sides are possibilities cannot be justified. Thus, many observers today contend that *no* nuclear warfare can ever be justified.

5. *Due proportion of means and ends.* No war can be waged with an anything-goes mentality. It is under this test also that many would declare a nuclear war unjust by definition, since the all-out use of nuclear weapons would destroy entire populations and endanger the survival of humankind.

6. *Just conduct.* Force, even in warfare, can be justified only to restrain an enemy from doing injury. When that can be done without killing (by taking prisoners or through nonfatal wounding, for example), the right to kill is removed. The use of weapons which cannot distinguish between combatants and noncombatants (nuclear, chemical, biological) is likewise ruled out.

7. *Mercy to the vanquished.* A defeated enemy must be shown mercy, including help with the rebuilding of what was destroyed. This means that

punitive reparations and the demand of unconditional surrender are not allowed.

Whether he knows the just-war teaching or not, the selective conscientious objector is following it, in some form or other. He is applying ethical criteria and making judgments. He is saying, "I do not object to all war, but find this particular war in which I am asked to take part to be unjust; I cannot in conscience join the effort."

Many religious groups in the late 1960s and early 1970s adopted official statements supporting the selective objection position. Most of them made these points:

1. Following conscience about participation in a specific war is not only honorable but required, and moral persons from the same religious tradition may come to opposing positions.

2. The United States government ought to change the draft law so that selective objection is accepted.

3. Even if selective objection remains unrecognized in law, the religious group is obligated to stand by its sons who conscientiously believe they must refuse to bear arms. They should expect to face the penalty required by the law, but their religious community must help them to live with that consequence.

Here are examples from two sources—neither of which is from a pacifist organization:

Roman Catholic Bishops Conference of the U.S. (1968). We . . . recommend a modification of the Selective Service Act making it possible, though not easy, for so-called selective conscientious objectors to refuse—without fear of imprisonment or loss of citizenship—to serve in wars which they consider unjust or in branches of service which would subject them to the performance of actions contrary to deeply held moral convictions about indiscriminate killing. (*Human Life in Our Day*, p. 44)

Lutheran Church—Missouri Synod (1969). Resolved, that the Synod affirm its historic theological position whereby it recognizes that conscientious objection to a war which an individual considers to be unjust is a valid theological stance. . . . Resolved, that the Synod petition the government to grant equal status under law to the conscientious objector to a specific war as it does to a conscientious objector to all wars. (Biennial Convention)

Since the end of inductions under the U.S. draft law, the churches have been relatively quiet about conscription and conscience, although the revival of draft registration in 1980 brought the issue back into consideration.

Most policy observers find it hard to envision Congress ever adopting a selective objection provision. They agree with the argument put forth by former Supreme Court Justice Abe Fortas in his book, *Concerning Dissent and Civil Disobedience*. Fortas points out that no state can view the particular-war objector in the same light as it views the all-wars objector. The state sees objection by a citizen to a particular war as a "difference of judgment or policy" rather than as an objection based upon primarily religious or moral concerns.[1] Once the government sets sail on a course of action, says Fortas, it needs and has a right to demand the support and cooperation of all crew members. It cannot exempt from duty those members who disagree with the direction the state is going.

"We may respect their sincerity and sympathize with their problem," Fortas writes, "but in fact their claim that their profound rejection of a particular war should prevail over the state's needs is hardly consistent with the basic theory of organized society. By participating in the particular war, the state takes the position that the war *is* justified and moral."[2]

In the Supreme Court's 1971 Gillette decision, a similar case was made in the majority opinion, written by Justice Thurgood Marshall. He made these central points:

First, it is the constitutional right of Congress to raise and support armies. This power would be jeopardized if selective conscientious objection were made legal. So many men might take advantage of the option that the necessary manpower would not be available to carry out government policies. Any state must maintain the power to protect itself.

Second, too much burden would fall on local draft boards if they were expected to decide who is and who is not sincere in his objection to a particular war. Unlike general objection, which must be based on absolute religious or moral grounds, selective objection is always based at least partially on more relative and political considerations. Local draft boards are simply not qualified to judge people on such a relative scale.

Third, Justice Marshall argued that since the nature of wars can change while in progress, an individual might judge a particular war to be unjust at one moment and then reverse his judgment at another time. The immoralities of any war are easily seen; the long-range morality of a war may be obscured.

Justice Marshall summarized by saying, "The nature of conscription, much less war itself, requires the personal desires and perhaps the dissenting view of those who must serve to be subordinated in some degree to the pursuit of public purposes."

Thus, the U.S. government's position continues to be: if you are selective in your objection, you must either submit to the will of the government or be willing to pay the price for violating the law.

THE ETHICAL IRONIES IN
SELECTIVE OBJECTION

There are two social-policy ironies that result from the selective objection position. One resides in the contrast between the general objector and the selective objector concerning the nature of their choice. The other appears in the strange philosophical position that the government is compelled to occupy because of its official policies on objectors.

1. The traditional conscientious objector starts from where he is now in time, looks backward and forward, and decides he can *never* participate in any war. He is entitled to legal exemption from military service. The selective objector also starts from where he is now in time, but concludes that he cannot definitely say what he could have done in past wars or what he will do concerning future ones. He considers it a ridiculous and meaningless exercise to try. He is not entitled to legal exemption from military service.

The irony is that the selective objector is penalized, in effect, for stating that there are occasions when he *would* bear arms for his country. He is penalized for disclaiming the absolute position of the pacifist and for trying to live with the ambiguities of decision making in a concrete situation.

2. The United States government finds itself perpetuating a second irony because of its contrasting treatment of the two kinds of objector. On the one hand, a position held by relatively few of our citizens, the pacifist or "all wars are immoral" position, is recognized as valid and provision for those holding it is written into the draft law. On the other hand, the view that grows out of religious traditions claimed by the vast majority of Americans is *not* recognized. One major reason, of course, has nothing to do with the merits of the two positions or the numbers of people subscribing to each, but rather flows from the very great practical difficulty of implementing any provision for recognizing selective objectors.

But there is a more philosophical reason as well. The pacifist is not questioning his own government's policy in entering a particular war. It is war *itself* that is the object of his rejection. The selective objector, however, is necessarily at odds with a specific policy of his government at a specific time, as Fortas argues. And that is a major reason why the government must be expected to continue saying no to selective conscientious objection. No government is likely to establish the precedent of setting aside the provisions of laws for any who claim they sincerely have a conscience problem with those laws. The danger of extension to other areas—payment of taxes, for example, or even traffic laws—is too threatening.

So we are likely to be living with these ironies for some time to come. And selective objectors will be living with the moral dilemma for just as long.

It is ethically troubling that we are in such a situation. The case can be made that the selective objector, who makes a careful judgment about a particular war, and then refuses participation on the basis of that judgment, is engaging more consciously and deliberately in moral conduct than is the absolutist. The one who philosophically or theologically is a pacifist is adopting the absolutist position that he can never, under any circumstances, engage in war—which puts the decision beyond the realm of moral judgment, in a certain sense. The sad dilemma is that the one who wrestles to a moral decision, the conclusion of which is not predetermined, is left with no legal place to stand. The one who does not need to undergo the rigors of moral decision is given a legal place to stand.

CHALLENGES TO THE RELIGIOUS COMMUNITY

The war/conscience debate poses a number of challenges to the religious community, whether or not people are being conscripted into military service. These challenges face especially those traditions in which the just-war ethic has dominated. They can be summarized under five imperatives.

1. *To give significant place to teaching the just-war criteria in religious nurture of both children and adults.* It can be safely estimated that the majority of members of just-war religious communities know next to nothing of the content of the teaching. It can be concluded because of the great number of members of nonpacifist religious groups who assume that one has two choices—and only two—when faced with a government's war policy: (1) the pacifist stance of opposition; (2) compliance with whatever policies or arguments the political leadership in power offers to the citizenry. There are few who organize their decision making and their citizenship around a third option—that of critical judgment based on ethical criteria such as the just-war teaching. In other words, few are those who act as though it is proper to oppose governmental military policies on a moral basis *other than pacifism*. In part, this can be attributed to a failure of the nonpeace churches to teach with any seriousness the ethic of war and peace which they say they espouse. The challenge from the pacifists is a just one: "If you are going to use an ethic other than pacifism to deal with war/peace questions, then *use* it, *teach* it, *apply* it. Don't leave peacemaking to the pacifists alone."

2. *To continue to support objectors of all kinds, including those who are outside the law.* Too often, the just-war religious communities have found it awkward, if not impossible, to support their own sons who run afoul of the law precisely *because* they followed the just-war teaching, which leads them

into selective objection. It is humanly understandable—perhaps—when religious communities are supposed to know something of the possibility of conflict between what is legal and what is moral, and supposed to know what to do when persons find themselves in such a bind. We are obliged to stand with such persons, to support them in every way possible (including pastoral care, counsel, financial help)—even if we do not, as a community, agree with each person's decision.

3. *To advocate that policy makers change the law, so that selective objectors may be treated in the same way general objectors are now treated.* (This is also a challenge to the peace churches, and they have generally supported recognition of selective objection.) It is not likely to be a successful effort, in the forseeable future. But the effort should be continued in any case. It is not unheard of in modern times that such a policy should be in place. Great Britain had a selective-objection system during the Second World War and it undermined neither the military strength nor the system of law generally. Perhaps SCO frightens the promilitarists precisely because few would use it during a defensive war situation, such as Britain's in 1940, but many would do so in a questionable military enterprise, such as the U.S. intervention in Vietnam.

4. *To apply just-war criteria to other citizenship roles, such as tax-paying.* If it is ethically proper to consider withholding my body from combatant purposes, it is just as proper to consider withholding my taxes which support military activities—at least those which appear to fall outside the just-war criteria. Such would include taxes for warfare that is not defensive, or taxes for weapon systems that do not meet the just-war tests (nuclear, chemical, biological). At least, there are many conscientious and thoughtful persons who are making that case, and the religious communities cannot avoid taking it seriously.

5. *To apply the just-war teaching to nuclear realities.* It appears to many that not only the use of nuclear weapons, but also the *threat* to use them, and their very *production* are violations of the just-war ethic. If that is to be taken seriously, the religious communities which espouse the just-war teaching would be called upon to consider: (1) a more aggressive witness to political leaders concerning the immorality of nuclear threats as a route to peace, (2) a more sophisticated analysis of alternative routes to global security, (3) a more intense pastoral ministry to those who work in the nuclear-weapons industry.

As applied to the question of *personal military participation*, both the traditional pacifist and the traditional just-war approaches are essentially negative in impact. "Let me out of serving because of my conscience, but someone else can go if his conscience does not object." And today it appears that the chief functioning application of either ethic is in relation to the matter of individual participation in military activity.

Both pacifists and nonpacifists badly need to shape ethical frameworks that can inspire religious adherents to positive peacebuilding. We need theologies of peacemaking which go well beyond the criteria on which individuals decide if they may submit to a draft. There are signs that both the peace churches and the just-war churches are moving toward the positive peacemaking task—in theology and practice. And none too soon. The war-prone world needs all the help there is, from any ethical well that has peaceful waters to be plumbed.

NOTES

1. Abe Fortas, *Concerning Dissent and Civil Disobedience* (New York: Signet Books, 1968), 104.

2. Ibid., 103.

9

A BIBLICAL APPROACH TO HUMAN RIGHTS

DONALD E. MILLER

The relationship of the churches to the question of human rights has been problematic in the twentieth century for several reasons. One reason is that the modern conception of human rights has its origin in the Enlightenment. One of the achievements of the Enlightenment was to describe moral realities in purely rational terms. The dependence upon reason alone is always suspect in the churches. A purely rational approach to morality tends to separate itself from the doctrine of God. Equally important is the disregard of human sinfulness in a purely rational approach to life.

Another problem churches have had with the human-rights tradition is the form in which those rights have been asserted. Whether in their assumption of intrinsic human freedom (the deontological view) or in their assumption of intrinsic individual self-interest (the teleological view), the human-rights tradition usually assumes both an individualism and an egoism that are suspect in the churches. The biblical concept of a covenant that is lifelong, with total loyalty, and entered into by a whole people, is considerably different from the individualistic ideas of a contract entered into by individuals under limited circumstances and with certain benefits in mind. In a similar way the biblical concept of love contrasts sharply with the ethical egoism that is usually assumed in the human-rights tradition. With the keeping of the rights contract all individuals stand to gain certain egoistic benefits. While the idea of love does not exclude the worthiness of the self before God, love contains elements of service and willingness to accept hardship that are not ordinarily a part of ethical egoism. Therefore

Donald E. Miller is professor of Christian Ethics at Bethany Theological Seminary, Oak Brook, Illinois.

the churches find it difficult to give their unqualified approval to those who insist upon their rights.

A third problem in the relationship of the churches to the human-rights tradition is raised by those proponents of human rights who stand outside the churches. Often the churches have not taken the lead in questions of human rights. Indeed the violation of the rights has often been given religious sanction. In the nineteenth century human slavery was justified by reference to Scripture, and in the twentieth century economic and political oppression are regularly given religious sanction. Evidences of racism and ethnic superiority may be as evident in the churches as in any other social institution. Critics of the churches are therefore understandably suspicious of church pronouncements about human rights.

A fourth problem in the relationship of the churches to the human-rights tradition is the great disagreement over just what is to be included within the concept of human rights. What may have been self-evident in the eighteenth century is not self-evident today. Even some of those founding American patriots who signed the human-rights Declaration of Independence did not free their own slaves. In our day there is great disagreement about whether economic rights are equally as important as civil rights. Some churches would speak out first for economic justice, and others would support political freedom before all else.

Still a fifth difficulty for the churches is the fact that the Bible says nothing directly about human rights. Certainly the Bible is not sanguine about what may be achieved in history, and often the Bible seems to condemn those outside Israel or the church. In what follows I want to show that the biblical perspective actually affirms human dignity in a very profound way. Nevertheless the absence of the concept of human rights in the Bible adds to the difficulty of the churches in relating to the human-rights tradition.

A sixth difficulty for the churches is the demise of the natural-law tradition. Behind the human-rights discussion lie fifteen hundred years of discussions regarding natural law. According to the doctrine of natural law there are certain moral tendencies in human societies that offer a sound basis for all legal and political decisions. For a community to disregard the natural law is self-destructive. This ancient moral concept of natural law is not to be confused with the modern physical and chemical concept of the laws of nature. Since the Reformation there has been an erosion of the concept of natural law (in the ancient moral sense), until in our day it is hardly ever defended. The modern idea of history has undercut the ancient idea that certain moral laws are fixed and unchanging. The churches' suspicion about natural law being limited to its own historical time carries over to human rights. The doctrine of human rights may also be an eighteenth-century fiction understandable in its own historical period.

A seventh difficulty, and perhaps the most basic, is that the relationship of the Christian gospel to any public policy has always been problematic. Jesus' admonition to "render unto Caesar what belongs to Caesar, and unto God what belongs to God" still leaves open the question of what belongs to Caesar and what belongs to God. Contradictory theories about public policy have developed in the history of Christianity, and each of those theories has tended to break down.[1] Some Christians have denied that the gospel has anything to do with public policy, and others have tended to sanctify whatever public policy is being followed at the time. With the millenia-long difficulty of churches relating to public policy, it is hardly surprising to find that the churches are mixed in their reaction to the human-rights tradition.

With these various difficulties standing in the way we might expect that the churches would be mixed, even confused, in their responses to the question of human rights in the latter decades of the twentieth century. The human-rights issue has probably achieved prominence in our time because of the United Nations declaration of human rights, and because of widespread awareness of human-rights violations around the world. Citizens are often given a choice between policies that support presumed self-interest, and policies that support presumed human rights.

The issue is admittedly complex, but the relationship of human rights to the biblical tradition is especially worthy of attention. If the churches are to achieve any kind of conviction about human rights, the analogies to the biblical tradition must be searched out. Certainly the belief of all Christian churches rests heavily upon interpreting the biblical tradition. Having said this, one is immediately aware that the biblical tradition is subject to many, often opposing, interpretations. Biblical scholarship has, however, made some steps toward agreements of interpretation that transcend denominational differences.

The question may be put this way: To what extent does the biblical tradition give support to the dignity of all humanity, such that liberty, protection, and a fair proportion of social benefits are to be guaranteed to all persons? From a biblical point of view moral values and obligations arise from a consideration of what human life and community are, what they mean, and what they are coming to be under God's providence and care. Biblically considered, God is the One from whom human community and values take on whatever ultimate meaning they have. Even the Enlightenment acknowleged the divine origin of human dignity with formulations such as, "All persons are endowed by their Creator with certain inalienable rights." Our question is whether such a view can be supported biblically, and whether the biblical perspective in any way alters the Enlightenment concept of human rights.

TWO BIBLICAL THEMES

Biblical scholarship of the Old and the New Testaments for more than a generation has emphasized the story of God's mighty acts in saving first Israel and then the church from slavery, oppression, sin, and death. Whether it is Moses and the Egyptian slave drivers, David and the Philistine oppressors, or Jesus and the power of Satan, God intervenes with a gracious action that saves and restores the people. Even though many may be lost, God saves the faithful few, establishing a covenant with them. The saving action of God is found from Genesis through Revelation, and so the Scripture is the story of God's gracious redemption of those who are a part of the covenantal community.

More recent biblical scholarship emphasizes a theme in Scripture that has received little attention by those who have seen in the Bible only the story of God's redeeming activity. The newly emphasized theme is that of God's creation and blessing.[2] According to the blessing tradition God has pushed back the powers of chaos to establish an orderly world. All humankind are blessed to the extent that they align themselves with the orderly processes of life. Blessing comes with a right relationship with the ongoing seasons and relationship of life. Nor is blessing limited to the few. Rather it is open to all humanity insofar as they are related reasonably and responsibly to the conditions of life.

Scholars have observed that the more particular story of God's redemptive activity is set within the general framework of God's creation and blessing of all humanity. Genesis begins with the establishment of a blessing (Gen. 1:26ff.), Revelation ends with the reestablishment of a blessed world (Rev. 22:1–5), and the blessing tradition appears throughout the Bible. The saving action of God and the blessing tradition are interwoven in the Bible so that when humanity loses the blessing through ignorance, arrogance, or rebellion, God intervenes and reestablishes a person, a family, and a community so that ultimately all humanity may again be blessed. The New Testament is related to the Old Testament in that in Jesus Christ we have a definitive personal expression of wisdom and blessing, and at the same time a definitive intervention of God to redeem humankind by establishing a new community of the faithful.[3]

Biblical support for human rights is to be sought first in the blessing tradition of God who creates and continually blesses humankind within the creation. When the blessing is lost, however, the life of Israel and the church, through the covenant initiated by God, becomes the new saving possibility for a fulfilled human destiny. The ideal values of Israel and the church are indicators of human destiny, even when those values are not lived out by the people. The struggle of Israel and the church to realize such values may offer a basis for a biblical attitude toward the struggle for human rights in our day.

BLESSING IN THE IMAGE OF GOD

Genesis 1—11 gives a brief account of the beginnings of all humankind before proceeding from chapter 12 on to trace the story of one particular family. Humankind is created within the orderly processes of nature but is formed in the image or likeness of God in a way that goes beyond anything else in the creation. The interpretation of the image of God has a long history, and the various interpretations reflect the various traditions from which the interpretations spring. Some traditions have emphasized human rationality which gives humankind the capacity to order life according to God's purposes. Others have emphasized the special capacity for communion with God. Recent commentators point out that a king's image or likeness in the ancient Near East was a seal that authenticated his announcements or proclamations. In this view all humanity is a sign or seal of God's rule of the creation.[4]

Without any doubt the image of God indicates that humanity has a special place in the creation. Psalm 8 is a commentary on the image of God, which image is a characteristic of all humankind and is not reserved for just a few. The image of God is all-inclusive and in no way qualified to exclude anyone. This powerful concept is the biblical basis for the dignity of all humanity. Human dignity is never something that is in question, nor can it be given or taken by any human action. Nor is it a gift of God to an otherwise insufficient creature. Rather human dignity is the very character of humankind, and is not capable of being obliterated.[5]

Recent scholarship points out that the characteristic of being both male and female is part of the image of God according to the text (Gen. 1:27). Being male and female is a special indication of human community, and that very relationship corresponds to the nature of God. The special dignity of humankind in creation applies to humankind as both male and female, so that neither male nor female may be considered to have less dignity than the other. Human dignity is also without regard to nature and cultural groupings, the origin of which is described in Genesis 10—11.

In the blessing tradition human life is preserved and deepened by the discernment and cultivation of right relationships with one another and with the environment and by the development of language and culture. The foolish, undiscerning person ignores or violates the God-established processes of life and loses the blessing. Then life becomes difficult, impoverished, and hard to bear. In the wisdom account the capacity of the environment to nourish an abundance of life is clearly related to cultivation of just relationships between humankind. In Genesis 4 Cain takes life from his brother, life that is given only by God. Abel's blood cries to God from the ground (v. 10) and the ground will no longer yield to Cain its strength (v. 12). Even so, God's gift of life is not taken from Cain (v. 15).

In the blessing tradition should God withdraw his support of life, then the unformed chaos will overcome human life and destroy it. This happens in the account of Noah. When God saw the wickedness of humans, God was sorry that he made them. The power of chaos is seen in the flood when "all the foundations of the great deep burst forth" (Gen. 7:11). God preserved one family, however, and established a covenant with "every living creature" (9:10), never again to permit the primal chaos to destroy life in that manner (9:8-17). This covenant with Noah becomes another statement of God's blessing and unconditional commitment to human life as well as its relation to animal life and the natural processes that support life. These affirmations serve to ground the dignity of human life.[6]

The messianic prophecies speak often in terms of the blessing of humanity. There shall come a time when wars end (Isaiah 9; 11; 26:12); prosperity will be without limit (Zech. 9:17; Isa. 65:16b-25; 66:11); contentment shall abound (Micah 4); and even the animals shall be at peace (Isaiah 11; 65:25). It is against such statements of blessing that the Beatitudes should be seen. In the Sermon on the Mount Jesus appeals to the natural processes as a guide to human attitudes about life (Matthew 6). Jesus also finds in the natural processes that sustain life an indication of the graciousness and justice of God to all humanity, even those who are unjust. In these ways Jesus is a teacher of the wisdom and blessing that is available to all humankind. Jesus Christ is furthermore the image of the invisible God (Col. 1:15) and in that fact the creation of humanity in the image of God is unalterably secured.

COVENANT AND HUMAN DESTINY

The Bible constantly points out that humankind does not live according to the possibilities for blessing that God has established. In the fall of humanity the image of God is distorted and the blessing severely diminished. Were it not for God's saving intervention humankind would be destroyed. That intervention is signaled in Genesis 12 by the covenant with Abraham. The fundamental saving event in the Old Testament is the exodus from Egypt, however, just as in the New Testament it is the death and resurrection of Jesus Christ. God chose Israel, who had no special claim to be saved. God then delivered Israel from Egyptian slavery and established a covenant with Israel at Sinai. Israel is to remember that one time they were in bondage and only by God's gracious redeeming act have they been freed. They were at one time no people, and now they have become a people.

Even within the salvation tradition the blessing reappears in the fact that Israel will prosper to the extent that the covenant is kept. The Old Testament declares that Israel is selected by God to be a blessing to the nations. So also in the New Testament is the church to be a blessing. In the covenants with Israel and the church one sees the possibilities of the renewal of human life in a time when life has lost God's blessing. We may therefore examine the various covenantal relationships within Israel as indicators of what proper human relationships are to be.

The relationship between the generations is fundamental for all humanity in the biblical view. God's gift of life is through the interrelatedness of the generations, whether at the animal or the human level. Children are therefore God's gift. Children are to honor their parents and parents are to attend to the upbringing of their children. Not reverencing the interrelatedness of the generations will lead to the loss of blessing.[7] Even though many actual problems occur in the relationships of the generations as recorded in Scripture, reverencing the relationship is basic to life itself. Part of the dignity of humanity under the covenant is that both children and the elderly have the right to care.

The relationship between masters and slaves is equalized in the liberation from Egypt, and also in the recognition that one God is creator of all.[8] Characteristically the Bible has simultaneous laws regarding the possession and treatment of slaves, the release of slaves, and the prohibition of slavery (Leviticus, esp. 25:39–40). The institution of slavery is acknowledged, even though God's act of liberating Israel from Egypt makes slavery intolerable (Lev. 25:42). In the holiness law slaves are to be released every fifty years (Lev. 25:8–9). Isaiah and Joel announce the coming release of the slave (Isa. 61:1; Joel 2:28–29). In the New Testament Pauline letters freedom from slavery is in Jesus Christ (Gal. 3:28), while the actual institution of slavery is still acknowledged (Philemon). Whereas slavery as an institution is acknowledged, it has already been overcome in principle in the exodus and in the cross of Christ. Humankind is seen to be in tension over the issue, but on the way to freedom through the outpouring of God's Spirit.[9]

The relationship to the neighbor is seen as a universally human problem in the Cain and Abel story (Genesis 4). Because of their different occupations, Cain and Abel are of different social and economic circumstances. The underlying enmity between brothers is a fundamental human problem. The same theme is picked up in the stories of Esau and Jacob (Gen. 27ff.) and Joseph and his brothers (Gen. 37:39ff.). Leviticus 19:17-18 asserts that "You shall not hate your brother in your heart," and "You shall love your neighbor as yourself." This very love of the neighbor requires that no one lend money to another Hebrew at a high rate of interest (Deut. 23:19-20). The poor and the slave are to be treated equally as brothers and sisters, as indeed is also the king.[10]

The stranger and sojourner is also to be considered as a neighbor (Exod. 19:33, 34) since all Israel was once a stranger and sojourner in Egypt. Even the enemy's need is to be considered. "If your enemy is hungry, give him to eat; and if he is thirsty, give him water to drink" (Prov. 25:21). The question of how to treat the sojourner and the enemy, with various opinions being given, becomes a central question in the Gospels. Jesus' story of the Good Samaritan is an example of the relation to the sojourner, and the Sermon on the Mount enjoins love of the enemy (Matt. 5:43-44). The Bible is realistic about actual hatred of enemies, but the direction of God's liberating reign is clear and is powerfully present in the person of Jesus Christ.

The relation between the teacher and the learner is considered basic in the Bible. Humankind are learners and life comes through learning the wisdom of the previous generation. Those who study the traditions of the fathers have great respect in Israel. Learning wisdom and blessing go hand in hand. Wisdom covers the whole conduct of life (Prov. 14:8). Wisdom is open to the accumulated experience of others (Prov. 28:26). By wisdom public life is rightly conducted. Wisdom is more powerful than might (Prov. 24:5). In justice the government rules powerfully.[11] In the New Testament the relationship of the disciples to the teacher is equally reverenced. The scribes and Pharisees in the Gospels are criticized not for their teaching, but for their failure to act according to their teaching (Matthew 23). Finally the beginning of all wisdom is the fear of God (Ps. 111:10). Because life is extended and enriched through learning, respect for the teacher-learner relationship is basic to human dignity.

The relationship of the powerful and the powerless, whether of the rich and the poor or of the rulers and the ruled, is basic to human dignity in the Bible. The text is clear that an important significance of the image of God in humanity is that God has given humanity the possibility and task of governing their own affairs. The forms of human governance are seen in their fallibility, however. The origin of Israel's monarchy is located not only in the divine anointing but also in the lust for power, according to Judg. 9:8-15, and in a desire to be like the other nations, according to 1 Sam. 8:5. The monarch in Israel originally had the utilitarian purpose of warding off the invasion of neighboring peoples. Saul, David, and Solomon are all criticized for assuming too much power (1 Samuel 13; 2 Samuel 12). Nathan the prophet's criticism of King David's execution of Uriah was in the form of a story of a rich man who stole from a poor man. Rather than appeal to tradition, Nathan appealed to the basic human dignity of the poor and the powerless in the face of the rich and the powerful. To disregard such human dignity is to "despise the Lord" (2 Samuel 12 NEB) and to lose the blessing.

After Solomon's death the elders counseled Rehoboam to be a servant to the people, but he preferred to increase the forced labor of the people (1 Kings 12:1-15). This led to rebellion and the division of the kingdom, that is, to the continual loss of blessing. Throughout Kings and Chronicles there is the admonition for no one to rob, cheat, or torment another person; even the king may not do these injustices. The king is rather to defend the poor, deliver the needy, crush the oppressor, and redeem life from oppression and violence (Ps. 72:2-4, 12-14).[12] The Pauline epistles and the Gospels have the same concern about the poor and the needy. The gospels portray Jesus as the king who stands in the place of the poor and the needy helping to carry their burden. The message of both testaments is that when human governments stay within the limits of human dignity, and when the rich and powerful do not oppress the poor, then the blessing will come to humanity.

THE BIBLICAL STANCE

In both the Old Testament and the New we have noted certain recurrent themes that are related to human rights.

1. God as both creator and redeemer has given a special, inalienable, and absolute dignity to all humanity, male and female, including all ages, races, social and economic conditions, and all national origins. The violation of that dignity constantly results in the loss of blessing and the debasement of human life.

2. The double commandment to love God and to love the neighbor is affirmed in both the Old and New Testaments even though the Bible is quite realistic about the extent to which humanity does not obey the commandment. The concept of love of enemies, most clearly formulated in the Gospels, presumes that no human being has lost the image of God.[13]

3. In the face of human violence, sin, and folly, God establishes a people

who will continue to testify to the possibility for human blessing, even when their own lives violate God's covenant. The coming of God's kingdom is a spiritual transformation in which individuals and their communities undergo a radical change. Such transformation is a continual sign of the dignity of all humanity. The Ninevites are also within God's purview (Jonah), and Christ has died for every person and every community.

4. The "servant mentality" of the exodus and of the resurrection calls believers to act and live toward love of all in spite of the fact that institutional practices, economic and social forces, and human perversity constantly thwart such expression. The resurrection and the Spirit of God are the quickening power developing a new and universal community under God's reign. Living not in the world as it now is, but toward the world as God intends it is the biblical stance. This means living and acting in all ways toward the kind of dignity in which humanity is created by God.

5. The Bible is very realistic about the depth of the resistance to God's righteousness. The Pauline epistles speak about the principalities and powers that govern human affairs. Scholars have argued persuasively that the principalities and powers represent the social, economic, and political forces that control a given historical period. The Pauline view is that these forces have been overcome in the death and resurrection of Jesus Christ and that their ultimate submission is now certain. If scholars have correctly identified the principalities and powers, then Christians are called to engage in the effort to do battle with the social, economic, and political forces that support the violation of human rights.

6. Whereas the Bible is clearly critical of other cultures at many points, for example, the condemnation of Baalism and Roman emperor worship, it is also highly respectful of the best in other traditions. It is generally thought that the primal history of humanity in Genesis draws heavily on non-Hebrew sources. The Pauline epistles are respectful of the best ideals of Greek and Roman as well as of Hebrew culture. This scriptural approval of wider human culture would seem to recommend to Christians a willingness to work with other traditions for the establishment of common definitions of human dignity in our time.

7. Both economic and political rights are affirmed in the Bible as a part of human dignity. They cannot be sharply separated from one another.

8. God has given the ongoing task of preserving human dignity within a life-supporting creation into the hands of humanity. To the extent that all humanity enters into that task, they will be blessed. Otherwise humanity will be cursed. To be engaged in such a task is to give praise to God, which is finally that for which humankind is destined.[14]

TO CONCLUDE

The summary we have given of the biblical account of human dignity contrasts in certain ways with the modern human-rights tradition. Let us conclude our discussion by looking at the ways that the human-rights tradition is either challenged or affirmed by the biblical perspective.

As we have already said, the Western human-rights tradition usually posits a certain intrinsic value to certain human capacities or to human nature as such. Those capacities may be variously stated as reason, freedom, or self-interest. The Bible testifies that all humanity reflects the divine dignity and worth through the image of God. In some sense humanity is an embodiment of the Holy One. In humanity God's image has been badly distorted, however, although not destroyed. Human immorality cannot erase the image of God, the sanctity of being human. The reflection of the divine dignity can be restored only through God's intervention, the establishing of a covenant that will potentially involve all people. Not humanity's intrinsic worth, rather the intrinsic worth of the Creator is the source of human dignity.

The human-rights tradition usually assumes a contract among parties or groups entered into for the mutual benefit of all parties involved. A variant way of speaking of human rights is in the rational capacity of all individuals to choose their own destinies. The Bible speaks of a covenant with God and among all the people. The covenant represents a total community commitment as well as a deep individual commitment. The covenant is more holistic and interactive than the individualistic human-rights tradition.

The human-rights tradition splits between political and economic rights. Western European countries insist upon political rights. Eastern European countries insist upon the priority of economic rights. The Bible sides with the powerless, whether political or economic. The powerless are to be empowered and the kingdoms of this world are to acknowledge the kingdom of God.

The rights debate often reflects the protection of class, national, or regional interest. America protests violation of human rights in Poland, but says nothing about violations of human rights in El Salvador. The Soviet Union does just the reverse. The Bible speaks from an acute awareness of the self-distortion of all of our claims. The new community, the kingdom of God, begins with confession, proceeds with embodiment of the covenant, and works from one saving intervention of God toward the next hoped-for intervention.

The West constantly wrestles with the question of whether political order and preservation against chaos demand terror or totalitarianism. The biblical history moves in the direction of discovering that terror and totalitarianism are both self-destructive. The reign of God will finally sanction neither, but the broken covenant will lead to either or both. God alone saves us from chaos.

The human-rights tradition presumes that legal and political processes give structure to the deeper moral claims of what is normatively "human." "To secure these rights governments are instituted among men" (Declaration of Independence). The Bible testifies that from the beginning of creation to the end of it, the creation has moral purpose. This moral purpose is embodied in covenant and law. The covenant is constantly broken, however, and the covenant cannot really be fulfilled unless there is a "will to care for the neighbor" among all of the people. This requires the Spirit of God to move and renew us.

The human-rights tradition assumes that the intrinsic value of the human is present in every individual human being, and therefore the claim of human rights is universal. The fact that rights are often not recognized or intentionally violated means that human rights are often an ideal rather than a praxis. In the biblical view the violation of the sanctity of the human is something in which we all participate through the "fall" of humanity. In Christ the sanctity of all humanity is reestablished, even though it continues to be violated. In Christ each person, even the enemy, becomes a neighbor, and in Christ a "will to care," a new spirit is released. Finally all the principalities and powers will be subject to Christ.

In the human-rights tradition there will be turmoil and revolution until human rights are guaranteed by law and deed. In the biblical view humanity moves toward a final judgment in which nations and individuals will be judged according to whether they respected the sanctity of humanity. Those who do so will be saved, and those who do not will fall under eternal judgment.

These contrasts show that the human-rights tradition is not a full embodiment of the biblical perspectives. The human-rights tradition is a secularized, individualized, historically conditioned analogy to certain themes of the biblical perspective. Human rights need to be deepened and enriched by the more holistic biblical view that goes beyond intrinsic self-interest or self-authenticating value to interacting, convenanting communities. One cannot expect, however, that the same religious vision will be shared by all people in our time. The Bible serves therefore not only to critique, but also to affirm the elements of a secular culture that give substance to human dignity. Just as the best in Babylonian, Egyptian, Hittite,

Greek, and Roman culture is affirmed and supported by the Bible, but within the purview of God's reign, so also the human-rights tradition of our time can be both challenged and affirmed within the ongoing reign of God.

NOTES

1. Ernst Troeltsch, *The Social Teaching of the Christian Church* (New York: Macmillan Co., 1931).

2. Walter Brueggemann, *In Man We Trust: The Neglected Side of Biblical Faith* (Richmond: John Knox Press, 1972). (The appendix contains an annotated bibliography of recent study of wisdom traditions.) Claus Westermann, *What Does the Old Testament Say About God?* (Atlanta: John Knox Press, 1979).

3. Claus Westermann, *The Old Testament and Jesus Christ* (Minneapolis: Augsburg Publishing House, 1968), 37ff., 69ff.

4. Hans Walter Wolff, *Anthropology of the Old Testament* (Philadelphia: Fortress Press, 1974), 160-61.

5. Westermann, *What Does the Old Testament Say About God?* 40.

6. Wolff, *Anthropology of the Old Testament,* 149.

7. Ibid., 177-84.

8. Ibid., 240.

9. Ibid., 204-5.

10. Ibid., 187.

11. Ibid., 206-13.

12. Ibid., 192-98.

13. G. Quell, "Love in the New Testament," in *Bible Key Words,* ed. J. R. Coates (New York: Harper & Brothers, 1951), 8-9.

14. E. Saunders, "The Bible and Human Rights," paper presented at the Seminar on Theological Assessment of Contrasting Human Rights Traditions, Garrett Theological Seminary, Evanston, Illinois, 4 November 1977 (Mimeographed). Wolff, *Anthropology of the Old Testament,* 223-28.

10
AN OVERVIEW WITH
STUDY QUESTIONS
JOHN OLIVER NELSON

War-peace-violence concerns used to be local—within a tribe, a clan, a family, a nation. In our century they have become, notoriously, global, civilization-wide, crucial for each living being and each descendant everywhere. So the agenda of these nine preceding chapters is as relentless, inescapable, and universal as any mandate can be.

The most drastic aspects of this war-peace-violence crux, as we are constantly reminded, take place in our own short generation. People are suddenly closer—tourists or television viewers or even genocidal strangers. Historic resentments flare fast. Compassion and philanthropy erupt just as quickly. Religion has become exportable, rapidly communicable, almost packaged. Have-nots are visually aware of haves. Motivation of leaders and groups is readily traced and publicized, as in "psychohistory." All in all, the lawyer's question to Jesus, "Who is my neighbor?" evokes answers heretofore unimaginable. Quite as insistent, especially for the mass media, is the uneasy, guarded query, "Who is my enemy?" Never before has there been such imminent urgency in the relation of peace, politics, and the people of God (whoever they may now be).

Unmistakably, some sort of peacemaking eagerness is struggling for expression among the general public, here and abroad. In the early 1980s, memorably and astonishingly, 750,000 or more marched in Manhattan for a multilateral nuclear freeze of weapons. Dozens of civil elections had this same freeze on their ballots. A half-million male teenagers, more or less, refused military registration. Editorials, congressional debates, student

---

John Oliver Nelson taught for many years at Yale Divinity School, chaired the Fellowship of Reconciliation, and founded Kirkridge, an ecumenical retreat center in Pennsylvania.

rallies, mothers for peace, veterans for peace, write-in campaigns, demonstrations were all part of an unprecedented worldwide stirring, which continues in dimensions unknown to previous history anywhere.

Specific religious aspects of this stirring, as the preceding chapters have copiously indicated, have become just as notable. Whole mainline Christian communions launched peace-war emphases, the most dramatic and controversial being the prophetic Pastoral Letter of American Roman Catholic Bishops. Dimensions of this awakening, as this book suggests, may make it as epochal as (1) missionary outreach in the nineteenth century, (2) the social gospel early in our own century, and (3) the ecumenical councils and mergers of the recent past. Jewish parallels in this country, and Buddhist ones abroad, have added interfaith angles to the broad picture.

Secular peacemaking and some of that found among church people may of course be leagues apart from religious "pacifism." The impulse behind mass concern has been almost purely self-preservation. It can be natural recoil from alarming threats against us and our children. Thus despite "love" placards borne by marchers, and reiterated even on millions of postage stamps, the rapid upsurge of the nuclear-freeze campaign was a call not for amity and understanding toward enemies, but a cry for security. Reasonable logic spoke here too: Is it rational to skimp on school lunches for tots in order to pile up redundant missiles? Authors of this book, even while sharing the almost universal nuclear foreboding of the times, have been marching to a distinctly different drummer—or even refusing to march at all.

All the volume's writers happen to be men. This is partly because up until now only men have had to make an actual military choice, and partly because few women had yet written in this field. Many nuclear-freeze advocates, too, would find these topics hopelessly recondite, parochial, and in-house, far upstream from "the ultimate consumer." It was said in scientific circles that World War II "had to end" when it did, because pure research in weaponry was exhausted. In some sort of parallel, "pure research in peace" is similarly now in urgently short supply.

Could these chapters "convert" anyone? It is unlikely. For the vast majority of us inherit our convictions about peace and violence whole. "He comes from a Mennonite family. . . ." "Her father is an army officer, so. . . ." "They are a campus intellectual household, vegetarians, so. . . ." "Her great-grandmother was a suffragette, so I assume she's a pacifist. . . ." "His dad got a purple heart in Korea, so he's gung-ho to enlist. . . ." Mindsets here are like those about politics and denomination.

Yet since World War II, people do come upon sighting-points for a change of peace-war conviction. People who take the New Testament seriously—in the succession of Gandhi or Martin Luther King, Jr., or Evangelicals for Social Action—have sometimes discovered new mandates there. Psychological study has prompted change also, when, for instance, insights of Carl Jung have pointed devotees to a new, inward, urbane nonviolence. History itself may convert: during the Vietnam War, some TV viewers were so revolted at battle carnage that they renounced military means. Nuclear scenes such as those in the TV drama "The Day After" have "converted" some.

In the other direction, violence has recently had reverse effects. Experience of a vicious mugging, terrorism, or group victimization has impelled countless Americans to reach for guns, advocate hanging, build acres of new cells, and vote for savage coercion and retaliation. Violence surrounds us as never before.

Against this series of brief side-glances, look at the succession of topics that are sharply dealt with in the nine chapters of this book: *Alan Geyer's* account of how churches (mostly Protestant) and church councils have pursued their way, often reluctantly, to deeper involvement in peace-war concerns; *Paul Peachey's* story—much of it not told before—of Protestant ecumenical but unofficial peace forces, working their way and shaping majority action; *Bryan Hehir's* tracing of Roman Catholic reappraisals of just war is similar exciting history written from within the bishops' deliberations themselves.

Following this, *Charles West* lifts out in perspective the Niebuhr-led changes in just-war thinking between World Wars I and II. Almost by contrast, an original account of the witness of historic peace churches (and any determined minority) is offered by *John Howard Yoder.* Then *James Childress* documents with the same sort of exactness the "pacifism" of the earliest Christians. Just war, the accommodating doctrine which succeeded such peace attitudes, is analyzed by *LeRoy Walters*, who outlines new perspectives of its history and logic. These logically point to recent conscientious-objector reasoning and legislation in a clarifying description by *Charles Lutz*, who also urges affirmative peace programs in churches— quite beyond the refusal decision. The topics end with *Donald Miller's* showing how human rights, here and worldwide, have become an issue of conscience, justice, and even resort to military violence.

Most of these clarifying reports carry over from the War-Nation-Church Study Group sessions (described in chap. 2) that prompted and gathered them, alongside dozens of related subjects. One observer of the interaction within this group marveled that it has been "the theological-ethical classroom of the peace movement." She further commented that in America peacemakers are usually so busy "making peace" that energy and time are lacking for deeper, long-term reasons and histories, so that the WANACH sphere of concern is all the more essential.

Responding to requests from study circles in churches and communities, a series of questions is provided here to build exchanges around the foregoing chapters. Such a series may also serve individual readers as an impressionist review of the various discussions:

1. *From Haunted Sleep to a New Awakening: The Churches and Disarmament in America (Geyer)*
   - Among the general public, has there indeed been misreading and wrong-myth-making about recent peace-war developments?
   - How do you explain church inattention to ACDA, ABMs, MIRVs, Non-Proliferation, SALT II?
   - Why since the early 1960s has there been veritable theology-ethics silence about both disarmament and nuclear violence?
   - Are listed peace "issues that now cry out" even more pressing this year?
   - Can we discern since the early 1980s a "new awakening" in the churches about peace-war? Awakening to what?

2. *Minorities with a Mission in the Churches (Peachey)*
   - Do most church members grasp the idea that first-century Christian life was pacifist? Why?
   - In empire centuries, how did the just-war doctrine evolve "as a largely futile attempt to discipline and to restrain"?
   - What motivated the peace societies and pacifisms of the nineteenth and early twentieth centuries?
   - In theology and ethics, were "Christian realism" and Niebuhrian just war in World War II years a special product of historical coincidence?
   - At "Oxford" and "Edinburgh" and in *Pacem in Terris* what engendered fresh peace stirrings again?
   - In what ways, if at all, was the prophetic work of A. J. Muste, the FOR, Church Peace Mission, and WANACH effective among the churches?
   - In what sense have ecumenism and the nuclear foreboding "resectarianized" the church?

3. *The Church-Type Revisited and Revised: The Case of the U.S. Catholic Bishops (Hehir)*

- Why was Vatican II on "Religious Liberty" the necessary precursor of the 1983 Pastoral Letter?
- How does "public church" differ from "political church," and how is the Letter "essentially a just-war analysis of the nuclear age"?
- If the Letter is "radically skeptical" that nuclear war can be controlled, how does it justify nuclear "deterrence"?
- Can the bishops maintain church-type dialogue with the secular state, and yet avoid "sectarian" criticism of its war policy?
- Addressing both the faithful and the civil-secular public, does the Letter speak from a different authority for each?
- How do you account for the shift from philosophical grounding in *Pacem in Terris* (1963) to more Scriptural-evangelical mandates in the Letter (1983)?
- Dealing with the four issues of abortion, human rights, nuclear strategy, and the economy, "there is a constant pull to move away from the church-type model toward either a more passive, nonpolitical position or toward a more confrontational, prophetic posture." Which does the Letter more clearly represent?

4. *Forgiven Violence: Christian Responsibility Between Pacifism and Just War (West)*
- If war is hell because it is unlimited and compelling, must it lay upon the believer a Lutheran "sin boldly" dilemma?
- Is Reinhold Niebuhr's role as "theologian of containment" and scourge of the self-righteous too subtle and subjective for most lay people?
- Does "balance of power" describe current American-Soviet competition, nuclear and otherwise?
- By what means today do enemies pursue "higher covenants of justice" above the level of their ordinary antagonisms?
- "Trusting risk," "humility [which] is a religious achievement"—are these possible in today's atmosphere of negotiation?
- Are Americans able, even after Vietnam, to acknowledge limits to our power, or to renounce some part of it?
- If, for the believer, war must be in some sense a "holy war," does this not open the door to jingoism and media manipulation?

5. *Neither Guerrilla nor Conquista: The Presence of the Kingdom as Social Ethic (Yoder)*
- Do we indeed share misleading public impressions of such words as

181

"minority," "sect," "establishment," even "peace church"?
- When minority becomes majority, does there inevitably follow a slackening of intense original conviction?
- Can radical Reformation actually mean restitution of what was primally and to a reclaiming of scriptural power and truth?
- Does church-against-world impatience really inspire many of us to break with the establishment?
- As dissidents seek to gather companions, is "the power of weakness" increased—or just the multiplicity of dissidence? Cite examples.
- What examples can you give of "the minority presence as conscience of society"? (The field of corrections is suggested.)
- Fitting topics for peace-church attention, the writer grants, are not the self-conscious problems of weakness vs. effectiveness, but rather "worship and servanthood, reconciliation and creativity." Do you agree?

6. *Moral Discourse About War in the Early Church (Childress)*
- Is Christian aversion to bloodshed, strong in the first centuries, still the core of conscientious objection today?
- Self-sacrifice, protection of the innocent, the sharing of corporate duty "exonerated" early Christians who went to war. Which is strongest now?
- Do lay people still believe clergy are "above" the demands of war, holier than ordinary folk? Is this changing?
- "The real evils in war are attitudinal, not physical, for the people killed would have soon died in any case." For Augustine, "The real evils of war are love of violence, revengeful cruelty, fierce and implacable enmity, wild resistance, and the lust of power." How does this classic manifesto apply to nuclear war?
- "The soldier is innocent, because his position makes obedience a duty." Do you agree? Can this relate to the statistic that more U.S. Vietnam combatants later committed suicide than died in uniform?
- Why are claims and examples early in history regarded as a more accurate response to the Sermon on the Mount than are our own?

7. *The Simple Structure of the Just-War Theory (Walters)*
- Augustine, dealing with Jesus' *pacifism*, argued that it referred only to intimate person-to-person nonviolence, not group action or war. Is this likely?
- For contemporary draft-resisters, is it the state's *authority* to conscript that is being resisted, or is there a higher reason?

182

- In current selective conscientious objection to war, is the criterion really whether the *cause* of the conflict is good or bad, the basic just-war query? Or is the selecting usually more complicated?
- What rules of *conduct* remain today? Does the range of permitted atrocity grow wider? Is imprecision, both in local terrorism and impossible nuclear holocaust, more and more taken for granted?
- Does classical, theologically deliberate just-war doctrine differ much from majority Protestant, Catholic, or even Pentagon limits and givens?

8. *Objection to Participation in Combat: Legality and Morality (Lutz)*
- Was American allowance for conscientious objection more generous in 1776 than it is now? Why?
- Why is it commonly claimed, as in Congress, that peacetime military conscription is inappropriate in America?
- What belief factors seem to have enlarged CO eligibility from required belief in a Supreme Being to more general grounds?
- What is the irony of refusing to allow selective objection while honoring general objection to war?
- As the nuclear threat involves civilians more than military personnel, what future form is conscientious-objector status likely to take?
- How do youth of predraft age, often surrounded with high-school military programs, become aware of their actual draft options?
- With both pacifist and just-war decisions mainly calling only for refusal, how can affirmative, active peace-seeking be advanced in churches?

9. *A Biblical Approach to Human Rights (Miller)*
- Why have church people, to date, seemed shruggish about human rights, near home or across the world?
- How do you account for erosion of regard for natural law since the Reformation? Do we no longer find any moral law fixed and binding?
- Would a "creating and blessing" account of God, rather than our traditional "redemptive" one, lift up human rights more strongly?
- In what way do these biblical concerns relate to human rights: covenant, freeing slaves, neighbor, stranger, learner, the weak, movement of the Spirit?
- How can it be said that the mission of human rights is the ground and empowerment of peacemaking?

Viewpoints explored in this book's nine chapters are those of a concerned "team" which is a minority within the church, Catholic or Protestant, which in turn is today certainly a minority within the world. Ernst Troeltsch discerned many decades ago in Europe that the great, half-concerned "church-type" membership loses its vitality without the small, gathered "sect-type" with its fiery dedication and eager fellowship. The authors here are such "evangelists" to the church at large.

Consider these writers as offering fresh insights, even historic ones. They speak within the wider family for whom peacemaking is a response to God. It is stark and timely meanings of "salvation" which they commend.